Non nobis, Domine!

The Convergence Movement
and
The Charismatic Episcopal Church

by

Mr. Hugh W. Kaiser
and
The Most Reverend Philip E. P. Weeks

CONTENTS

ACKNOWLEDGEMENTS!

We wish to express our thanks to the Most Reverend Loren Thomas Hines, Archbishop of the Province of Southeast Asia, whose invitation to instruct Filipino churches in The Convergence Movement as they prepared to come into the Charismatic Episcopal Church made possible the initial Manual for Convergence that later resulted in this book.

We also express our thanks to the Most Reverend Dale Howard, former Archbishop for the International Development Agency, the missionary arm of the International Communion of the Charismatic Episcopal Church, for his encouragement. It was through his desire that the Manual for Convergence might be translated into German for use with merging churches in Europe that gave us the incentive to expand the Manual into narrative form. It was never translated into German, but it formed the basis for the first publishing of *"Non nobis, Domine!"*.

We further thank all those who have sat under our teaching, not knowing they were making possible this book, as we learned more and more in our effort to answer the questions they had concerning The Convergence Movement. Over the years of Barnabas Ministries, Inc. work in the Philippines, teams of people shared in the teaching. Some portions of teaching included in *"Non nobis, Domine!"* were contributions of team members, among whom were Father Geoffrey Schimitt and Father Bruce Simpson. This is a compilation of teaching God provided through faithful servants woven into the complete story of Convergence as we tell it. We apologize if we have failed to acknowledge others who may have given teachings to later appear in these pages. The neglect is not intentional, but the result of poor aging memory.

A great contribution to the history of CEC has been made by former Archbishop Randy Sly who was part of the early beginning.

Had it not been for the numerous contributors to Barnabas Ministries, Inc. under the direction of Bishop Weeks, we would never have been able to go into the many places God prepared for us to teach. The contributions to BMI, Inc. by many supporters financed our trips in the Philippines, Europe and Africa.

We praise Almighty God for the opportunities He has opened to us to share our understanding of The Convergence Movement with congregations in the United States, the Philippines, Europe and Africa.

We give thanks to Len Rogers who did much of the proof reading, correcting typos from the first edition, and to Melanie Weeks Stern for her tremendous assistance in formatting this edition for publication.

Scripture quotations come from the King James Version of the Holy Bible, and from The Holy Bible, New International Version (North American Edition), copyright ©1973, 1978, 1984 by the International Bible Society. Quotes from the New International Version are used by permission of Zondervan Publishing House.

Non nobis, Domine, sed nomini tuo da gloriam! AMEN [Psalm 115: 1]

Hugh W. Kaiser
Philip E.P.Weeks

INTRODUCTION

In 1977 a gathering of evangelical clergy occurred in Chicago, Illinois. They believed the Holy Spirit orchestrated the meeting. From independent and denominational backgrounds strongly evangelical in emphasis, they came to consider how they could impact the United States with the Good News of a Savior named Jesus.

To the amazement of each participant, the Holy Spirit had a different agenda. They were to consider each other, in the words of St Paul to the Philippian Church, as more esteemed than they, and in the admonition of the hour, pastors humbled themselves before each other in order to receive what each had to give the other.

The Chicago Gathering was for a few pastors and churches the beginning of a journey that would cause them to return to the future. It would take them back across years to the root of the Jesse tree, and discover their roots in historical Christianity. For many of them this was new. They had little consideration of the existence of the Church prior to their own conversion. They discovered that the Church had withstood years of trials and tribulations, somctimes swaying from the basic Kerygma of the historical Church, but always with a corrective action by the Holy Spirit, a remnant remained.

In the mid-1980s evangelical-charismatics began to be led by God to study liturgy. There were different men who sought the richness of liturgical worship. Some came into the Episcopal Church; some went into the Antiochean Orthodox Church. Some formed their own group. Among those searchers God led Randolph Adler of San Clemente,

1

CA, and Joseph Moats of Tucson, AZ, two independent charismatics to search and explore the roots of the Church, especially liturgical and sacramental matters.

The name ascribed to this journey of some clergy is **The Convergence Movement**. The excitement of this movement is in the discovery of historical practices of the Church by men who previously had rejected those practices as non-essential. Those who have dared to pursue this journey have not only discovered other emphases in Christianity, but also have come to a deeper appreciation of their own particular emphasis. Three streams or emphases in Christianity merge in The Convergence Movement:- evangelical, Pentecostal and catholic.

Non Nobis, Domine! is the story of such a journey by two men God used, who discovered their historical roots in Jesus Christ as the Founder of the Church, and the Rock upon which His Church is built. They have not been alone in this journey, but the unique way in which God worked in the lives of these two men deserves to be told, for through them a new move of God is taking place and has been expressed in the fast growing Charismatic Episcopal Church.

Our story reveals the uniqueness of the Convergence Movement, and how this new move of God is manifesting itself in the Charismatic Episcopal Church throughout the world.

The content herein is the expanded version of an earlier produced **Manual For Convergence Outreach Seminar** which has been used in outline form for teaching about Convergence, and the Charismatic Episcopal Church in congregations, first in the Philippine Islands, and subsequently in Europe and Africa as well as the United States of America. No doubt there is much more to be said about the theology of Convergence, and the glorious opportunities God is providing His Church. We realize we have barely begun to tell the story. However, it is our prayer that the reader will more fully understand what God is doing, and may be better equipped to tell the story to others. As indigenous leaders are trained, this book may serve as a guide to the preparation of national manuals.

The Most Reverend Philip E. P. Weeks
The Charismatic Episcopal Church

Feast of the Holy Cross, 1998 – Original Manual For Convergence

The original manuscript has gone through a major revision in the first chapter IN THE BEGINNING. Some of the historical data as told to us we later found to be inaccurate, and incomplete, therefore some of the original script has been deleted.

Revised November 1, 2011 All Saints Day

APPRECIATION

Austin Randolph Adler – Founder and First Patriarch

We are indebted to Bishop Adler for his sacrifice in the anti-abortion witness that precipitated the birth of the Charismatic Episcopal Church, and the leadership he gave to the development of this communion, its expansion in America, Africa, the Philippines and Brazil. Because of his vision, the Charismatic Episcopal Church stands prepared to fill the void that exists in many mainline Protestant and independent churches.

IN THE BEGINNING

At the outset let us stress that the Charismatic Episcopal Church is not a breakaway or schismatic denomination. It did not come from any existing denomination. It is a new move of God that some believe could be His way of fulfilling the prayer of Jesus in John 17:21 (KJV): *"That they all may be one; as thou, Father, art in me, and I in thee, that they also may be one in us: that the world may believe that thou hast sent me."*

In May1977, dialogue began amongst evangelical and charismatic independent clergy regarding their need for networking and inter-communion, and a prophetic call for evangelicals to rediscover their roots in historic Christianity. In the mid-1980s evangelical-charismatics began to be led by God to study liturgy. There were different men who sought the richness of liturgical worship. Some came into the Episcopal Church in the United States of America such as an Assembly of God congregation in Valdosta, Georgia. Some went into the Antiochean Orthodox Church. Some formed their own group. Among those searchers God led Austin Randolph Adler of San Clemente, California, and Joseph Moats of Tucson, Arizona, two independent charismatics to search and explore the roots of the Church, especially liturgical and sacramental values.

At a Conference on Prophecy in Naples, FL in the early 1990s, a Word was given to two conference participants. ***GOD IS GOING TO USE YOU TO DO A NEW WORK!*** That prophecy was given to Randolph Adler and Joseph Moats. Bishop Moats related the experience to me one evening in Denver, Colorado, on the eve of an ordination. He and Randy Adler were long time

5

friends and golfing buddies. They heard of this conference in Florida and attended it. They had no understanding of what the prophecy meant, and following the conference, returned to their respective places, monthly getting together for a game of golf, sometimes in California and alternate months in Arizona.

During one of their monthly golf games following the conference, Randy asked Joe what God was saying to him. "Nothing special," replied Pastor Moats, upon which Adler handed him a piece of paper on which a scripture had been written. Moats said he forgot about the paper, and several weeks later, back in his church in Tucson, discovered the paper in his trouser pocket. He opened and read it. It was Ezekiel 22: 26: "My *priests have violated my law, and have profaned mine holy things: they have put no difference between the holy and profane, neither have they showed difference between the unclean and the clean, and have hid their eyes from my Sabbaths, and I am profaned among them.*" -(KJV)

After reading this, Pastor Moats was prostrated by the Spirit. As he lay on the floor, in prayer, he asked the Lord, "What are the holy things the priests have profaned that now You are profaned?" God gave him seven things: **Baptism, The Lord's Supper, Confirmation, Penance, Unction, Holy Matrimony,** and **Holy Orders - The Traditional Seven Sacraments of the Church**. These were practically unknown to this minister of a Nazarene Church background. He began to read in order that he could *"teach my people the difference between the holy and profane, and cause them to discern between the unclean and the clean"* [Ezekiel 44: 23 KJV].

Bishop Moats tells his personal journey that parallels that of other men who have come into the Convergence Movement from non-liturgical churches. As he read books on liturgy, he discovered that the worship of the early Church came directly from guidelines given in the Old Testament. He learned that those who were called to minister before the Lord were directed to wear certain type clothes that distinguished them from the ordinary worshipers. Over the years, these robes called vestments, took on special form and meaning as setting apart those who ministered in the Church. The vestments not only made certain distinctions between the worshiper and the leaders of worship, but they also gave meaning and emphasis to the visual response of the worshiper as to what ministry was being offered before the altar of the Lord.

Bishop Moats went to an evangelical bookstore in Tucson inquiring if they had special robes for clergy, and made his first purchase. The next Sunday he entered the pulpit wearing his new clerical robe. One might imagine his congregation was slightly confused as to what was happening to their pastor. As he read on he learned that clergy wore some kind of cloth called a stole. Back to the evangelical bookstore he went inquiring about stoles. The manager wanted to know what color he wanted. Bishop Moats did not know there were various colors. Understand that this was many months prior to his consecration as a bishop. He was a pastor of a non-denominational charismatic church he formed after the Nazarene Church defrocked him because he received the baptism in the Holy Spirit.

When he learned there were four different colors in the liturgical year, and the bookstore manager had four different colored stoles, he chose the green one because it was to him the prettiest of the lot. The next Sunday he walked in wearing the stole with absolutely no understanding of its meaning. Nevertheless, this was the faithfulness of one who wished to please God, and restore those things God had revealed as having been profaned. In New Testament language one would say Joseph Moats was willing to be a fool for Christ's sake.

Bishop Adler's story is somewhat different. In the 1970s, he had been a street preacher with a heart for souls in Orlando, Florida. Later he moved to San Clemente, California, and assumed the pastorate of a charismatic church. God revealed to him the tragedy and sin of the United States in legally permitting the killing of unborn babies, and while it was legal by United States law, it was unlawful by God's law. He and his congregation became active in the anti-abortion move, and on several occasions when arrested and imprisoned, he noticed the Roman Catholics, who also were arrested for demonstrating, were praying while the charismatics were questioning God as to why this awful thing had happened to them. As evangelical-charismatics they had often questioned the validity of Roman Catholicism, and if the people really were Christian. Unlike themselves, he realized that these Roman Catholics had a depth of spirituality his evangelical followers lacked. God placed a hunger in his spirit. He began to read church history, and found a new kinship with the early Church Fathers and their writings. His study of liturgy was passed on to Joseph Moats as they walked the golf course, and together God groomed these men for the new move He was about to do.

8

In a very real way the Charismatic Episcopal Church was birthed through the anti-abortion movement when Adler and members of his San Clemente congregation were beaten by the Los Angeles police, and jailed because they sought to save the life of the unborn. The Charismatic Episcopal Church has not shirked its responsibility in caring for the unborn, and in the spirit of the founder and members of St. Michael Church, advocates the sacredness of human life embodied in the unborn. CEC For Life is a major ministry throughout this Communion.

Major Kenneth P. Tanner was killed in Vietnam leaving a wife and several children. Randolph Alder met and married Mrs. Tanner, and it was son Kenneth who greatly encouraged his step-father to study liturgy. Kenneth was a student at Oral Roberts University, and was captivated by the works of ORU's Chaplain Bob Stamps. Not enough is known about the tremendous influence Kenneth Tanner had upon Randolph Adler by encouraging him to attend an Episcopal Church, and opened the door of convergence that eventually led to the formation of The Charismatic Episcopal Church. Kenneth is now a priest in the Charismatic Episcopal Church.

Subsequently, the International Communion of the Charismatic Episcopal Church was formed with the consecration of Randolph Adler as bishop June 26, 1992. This was the first formalized expression of the Convergence Movement. Joseph Moats and Delmer Robinson, instrumental in arranging Bishop Adler's consecration, were consecrated bishops at a later date. Bishop Robinson was named *bishop emeritus,* and never actually functioned in any official capactiy as a bishop.

God made the choice between the two men as to who would be primary in leadership. It was clear to Bishop Moats that Bishop Adler should be the primary bishop of the church, and it was later confirmed when Bishop Moats suffered an extended illness that in its infancy, had he been the Primate the Charismatic Episcopal Church might never have been established.

The Charismatic Episcopal Church in America began with three congregations. Bishop Adler one day asked Bishop Moats if God might give them ten congregations by year 2000. God, however, had other plans that would have staggered the imagination of these founding fathers had He revealed it to them at the time. By 1998 more than 500 churches composed an international communion that includes churches in Africa, Europe, Asia and North America. The majority of the churches that compose the International Communion of the Charismatic Episcopal Church are congregations that once were independent, charismatic and evangelical. About twenty percent have come from established denominations. Today this communion continues to grow in Brazil, the Philippines, Europe, and throughout Africa. What began from the prison cell in Los Angeles as believers sought to save the life of unborn children, has given life and hope to thousands embracing a fullness of the Christian Faith.

Wayne Boosahda, who became a Bishop in the Evangelical Episcopal Church, and Randy Sly who became a Bishop in the CEC, wrote an article on the Convergence Movement in "Worship Today" magazine in the early part of 1992. The article was later incorporated by Robert Webber in his "Complete Encyclopedia of Christian Worship". It caught the eye of Bishop Adler, and Sly was contacted by Adler and invited to visit San Clemente. He was ordained as the first priest in CEC outside the original three churches. An article in "Ministries Today" by Paul Thigpen about the CEC brought a hugh influx of inquirires, and growth began.

The first major conference was held in Oklahoma in 1993. It was called the St. Barnabas Conference and was designed as a meeting place for many of those who were discovering the Convergence of Streams, and coming from Evangelical, Charismatic, Roman Catholic, Orthodox and Episcopal jurisdictions. Speakers included Bob Stamps from ORU, Peter Guilquist of the Antiochean Orthodox Church, Robert Webber and Thomas Howard. Several clergymen from the CEC were present. This conference might be considered as the "seed" of the Convergence Movement in America.

It should be recognized that the International Communion of The Charismatic Episcopal Church was the first formalized expression of the Convergence Movement. However, at the same time, individual churches and pastors were on a similar journey, and not limited to men in America. About this same time an Assembly of God clergyman in the Philippines, Loren Thomas Hines, had begun to be led by the Holy Spirit into a study of the historical church and othodoxy. He had already begun the transition from informal worship to liturgical worship in the congregations under his leadership when he met Bishop Adler at a conference in the United States. A few months after his consecration as a Bishop in 1993, Randy Sly visited the Phiippines, and reported back to Bishop Adler that had they not already organized the CEC, they should have joined Tom Hines. He had already started a strong Convergence Movement in the Philippines. Rather than both doing virtually the same thing, Hines decided to unite with Adler, and he was named Primate over the Asian work which also included Hines' Filipino groups in various European countries. CEC became an international move of God.

According to Wikipedia's accounting, Pentecostal scholar H. Vinson Synan, the International Communion of The Charismatic Episcopal Church (ICCEC) was the first to use the word "charismatic" in its official name.

The task ahead is to maintain a balance of the three streams of Christianity. Many times when a church seeks respectability they lose the Spirit of God. God will not share His Glory with man, and if a Church desires the acceptance and approval of men, God will not abide. There are countless stories in church history of movements inspired by the Holy Spirit only to be thwarted when men fail to patiently listen to God.

The Charismatic Episcopal Church need not use the out grown methods and techniques of the evangelical and full gospel churches in presenting the vital claims of Jesus to the world. The Convergence Movement captivates the fullness of the Gospel as demonstrated in the proclamation of the Good News in the Power of the Holy Spirit, and celebrated as the People of God in corporate worship as historically given to the Church. The Convergence Movement reflects the unique merger of the orthodox-catholic [liturgical-sacramental], evangelical, and Pentecostal-charismatic lines of the Church.

Congregations entering the Charismatic Episcopal Church must be thoroughly knowledgeable of the Convergence Movement. Evangelical Churches **must** embrace the Pentecostal and Liturgical-Sacramental aspects of Convergence. Pentecostal-charismatic churches **must** discover the vitality of a living worship in Liturgy. Liturgical-sacramental churches **must** embrace the evangelical and charismatic expressions of the Christian life. The uniqueness of the Charismatic Episcopal Church is its balance to embrace all three expressions or streams of the Church.

In the years 1995, 1996, 1997, 1998, Hugh and Philip helped the International Communion of the Charismatic Episcopal Church in the Philippines, and the Filipino Confederation in Europe, develop the fundamental principles and operational details of the Convergence Movement through outreach programs by teachings on:

a: Preaching a simple salvation message followed by invitation to a personal relationship with Jesus

b: Teaching on the Baptism in the Holy Spirit, and prayer for those who wish to receive a fuller measure of the Holy Spirit for ministry

c: Teaching on basics in liturgical worship, and the place of sacraments

In 1998, Bishop Weeks was called to Africa where these principles were taught men coming into the Charismatic Episcopal Church from the Anglican Communion, and independent denominations.

The material that follows may be used by Church leaders to form the basis for seminars, individual informational reading, or directed study, for those interested in learning more about the Charismatic Episcopal Church. Each time we have conducted a seminar, the Holy Spirit reveals more to us that ought to be included in our teaching. Our original Manual has gone through numerous revisions, reflecting upon these new revelations. When training indigenous leaders, a Manual for that particular country or region may be prepared. We pray, however, the content herein may serve as a guide for fuller understanding of the beliefs and practices of the Charismatic Episcopal Church.

There will be times when we will simply list scripture references, and other times we will print the scripture in the text of this book. Where we have only given the references, please take the time to search out those verses in your Bible. Through this way we more readily understand what God is doing.

CEC Logo For The American Church

The three symbols represent the divisions (or streams) of the worldwide church.

The top symbol is wine, representing the Sacramental churches where the faith is maintained through its clergy, rituals and creeds.

The middle symbol is an open Bible, representing the Evangelical churches where the Bible, and the need for a personal faith in Jesus Christ as Savior and Lord, is emphasized.

The bottom symbol is a flame, representing the Charismatic churches where the supernatural gifts of the Holy Spirit are emphasized.

The framework reveals three more symbols; a cup, an altar and a fireplace.

The cup holds the wine so we can receive it. The altar supports the Word so we can rightly discern it. The fireplace holds the flame so we are safely warmed by it.

When turned on its side the framework reveals the three letters…C E C. These stand for the Charismatic Episcopal Church.

Back To The Future

Our teaching about Convergence began in the Philippine Islands with Archbishop Loren Thomas Hines in 1995. Barnabas Ministries had at that time worked in the Philippines for fourteen years, and understood some of the uniqueness of the island culture. We made a proposal to work with the Charismatic Episcopal Church in the Philippines as evangelical and charismatic congregations under Bishop Hines former ministry were coming into the Church. They primarily needed teaching on liturgy and sacraments, but we developed a seminar format that allowed re-enforcement of the evangelical and charismatic streams of the Church as well as educating them on the liturgical-sacramental aspects which they had rejected..

Many of the groups under the Christian Life Fellowship had come from a Roman Catholic background. Some evangelical pastors had taught them that all things pertaining to the Roman Catholic Church were evil. Even good things about the Church had been renounced. Bishop Moats once said his Arizona church observed the Lord's Supper several times a year, "If we could work it into our charismatic worship." This was the attitude of these Filipino churches.

In one place the new Charismatic Episcopal Church priest said his people were questioning him extensively about things they once practiced as Roman Catholics, and then had been told those things were not of God, but now being told it was proper to do them. Confusion reigned! And our assignment was to help overcome this confusion, and re-establish those things that were good, but now give them understanding. We found that many Christians have

17

no idea why they do certain things in church; they copy other people, or they have always done certain things without knowledge as to the meaning.

These believers needed to understand the existence of the Church prior to their own personal encounter with Christ, and what was a proper relationship with the Church. The Church has twenty centuries of history, good and bad, nevertheless, continues to fulfill the promise of Jesus to withstand the assaults of the devil and block the gates of hell.

Jesus Christ founded the Church. *"For where two or three are gathered together in my name, there am I in the midst of them."* [Matthew 18:20 KJV] This is the earliest definition of what the Church is - the people in union with Jesus Christ. This pre-dates the day of Pentecost. There were many times when the Church is visible prior to Pentecost because Jesus was gathered with His Disciples. He gave them authority and power over Satan prior to the empowerment imparted upon the Church on Pentecost, but appeared to be a "temporary" power until after His glorification.

On the Day of Pentecost the gathered one hundred and twenty believers were empowered by the Holy Spirit as promised by Jesus, and the Church was officially born. From that wonderful event in Jerusalem the Church grew. It went through times of persecution as well as times of peace and prosperity. Many of those Jews, who were scattered to other nations because of the Roman invasions of Titus and Vespasian, and the eventual fall of Jerusalem in A.D. 70, took the Church with them into these foreign lands. The first Christians were Jews who believed that Jesus was indeed the Messiah Israel had longed to receive.

The Episcopacy and Diaconate, and the development of the priesthood, came as early as the first few years after the Ascension of Jesus. The Greek word *"presbyteros"* appears in the Acts of the Apostles [Acts 14:23 translated as elder] and the Greek *"episcopos"* [translated as bishop] in the epistles of St Paul to 1 Timothy 3:1-2, and Titus 1:7. The Diaconate was established by the first Apostles and recorded in the Acts of the Apostles [Acts 6:3]. The government of the early church operated within Councils as the Holy Spirit directed the Apostles, and consensus confirmed the Voice of the Spirit spoken through the Bishops [Acts 1:13-15; 6:2; 13:1-3; 15:1-29]]. Government by consensus on the national level [the House of Bishops], on the Diocesan level [the Bishop and priests], and on the local church level [the priests and deacons with a council of men chosen by the priest] constitutes a "founding principle" of the Charismatic Episcopal Church. Our founders believe the Church is a Theocracy rather than a democracy, and decisions are made after many hours and sometime days of prayer.

By the fourth quarter of the second century Apostolic Succession was commonly accepted. St Polycarp, successor of St John the Divine, said Christ gave specific instructions to St John on how their successors were to transmit faithfully and accurately what had been taught them by Christ, and in appointing bishops as their successors, they maintained an unbroken line of authority. Irenaeus, bishop of Lyons, was also instrumental in establishing apostolic succession.

A failure we have found among many evangelicals is they do not realize the Church determined what books were to finally be included in the Holy Bible. The Canon of the New Testament was finalized by the end of second

19

century. In a letter from Athanasius, Bishop of Alexandria 367 A.D., twenty-seven books in the New Testament is listed as accepted.

With the conversion of Emperor Constantine and Empress Helena in A.D. 313, Christianity was made legal and marked the end of violent legalized persecution. In A.D. 314 the Council of Arles was held and in attendance were three bishops from what we today know as the British Isles. This is important to note because it speaks of the spread of Christianity prior to its being legalized. In A.D. 325 the Council of Nicea was held out of which came the Nicene Creed as the test by which all teachings could be judged. The original version did not have the *filioque*, which got added by some westerners because Athanasius had included it in his creed. This is the statement that the Holy Spirit proceeds from the Father *and the Son*, the latter being the *filioque* clause. This is still a controversy between the Eastern and Western Churches. Most of the Western Churches insert the *filioque* clause while the Eastern Churches omit it. The Charismatic Episcopal Church has omitted the *filioque* from the Nicene Creed. Because of opposition in the Philippines to things that resemble the Roman Catholic Church, the Filipino Charismatic Episcopal Church has adapted some parts of the Eastern [Orthodox] style of worship and practice.

It is believed that the commonly called Apostles Creed was a baptismal statement that precedes the formulation of the Nicene Creed. The Nicene Creed was formulated to protect the Church against heresy. The Apostles Creed was a simple statement of Faith ascribed to by those being baptized. Bishop Adler emphasized that recitation of the Nicene Creed following the Sermon in the Order of the Eucharist is comparable to entering into spiritual warfare against Satan. The Word of God has been proclaimed in the readings of the scriptures. The preaching of the sermon is followed by the historical declaration of what the Church believes, and Satan's strongholds are challenged.

With the growth of Christianity, the leadership believed that more efficient organization was required and, hence, the Papacy was developed. St Peter was considered the first bishop of Rome, followed by Linus, and thirdly, Clement, with others following according to Irenaeus. Eusebius, a fourth century historian, gave a list of bishops as evidence of a succession of bishops from the apostles, assuring that the Gospel has been conserved and handed down. This was considered to be Apostolic Succession, a very important part of the government of the Church that gives to the contemporary Church an unbroken line to the early Church and Jesus himself.

In A.D. 596, the Bishop of Rome sent St. Augustine to Canterbury in England, but the Church was already in Britain, and on his arrival, a Frankish Bishop met Augustine. The main difference was the date of celebrating Easter; decided at the Council of Whitby 607 A.D. which brought the British Church into communion with Rome. The early existence of the Church in England is important for it shows the missionary outreach and expansion of the Church before the Pope sent St. Augustine to England.

Prior to A.D. 1054 there was basically only ONE Church. Of course, there were different expressions of the Church's corporate life as reflected in the areas where she is established, but there remained one undivided line to Jesus Christ as the Cornerstone. It is erroneous to speak of the Roman Catholic Church prior to this date when a major division occurred. The main issues that culminated the division were the authority of the Bishop of Rome, and the date for Easter. The Patriarch of Constantinople held that he had equal authority with the Bishop of Rome, who claimed greater authority because he succeeded St. Peter. Because of this controversy, the first division occurred, separating the Eastern [Orthodox] Church from the Western [Roman Catholic] Church, causing bitter conflict to this day.

In his effort to build a Basilica, the bishop of Rome in the first years of the sixteenth century, devised a money-raising scheme where people were told that they could purchase the soul of loved ones from Purgatory. Purgatory was a corrupted teaching about the "place of the dead" developed for sordid gain. By giving money toward the building of the Basilica, they could shorten the time of those in Purgatory and speed their way on to heaven. Martin Luther, a priest in the Roman Church, cried "foul". He struggled with what he considered to be a violent misreading of Holy Scripture, and in 1517 posted his 95 Theses on his Wittenberg Church door, declaring, *"the just shall live by faith."* [Rom 1:17 KJV] It was the battle cry for the Reformation that later found support from reformers like Zwingli and Calvin. It was at the same time, but for very different reasons, that Henry VIII of England declared the separation of the Church in England from the authority of the Pope, and declared himself as the "head" of the Church in England. John Wesley capped the list of reformers with his Aldersgate's "heart warming" experience on May 24, 1738, and when the Bishop of London would not ordain Wesleyan pastors for ministry in the new America, Wesley took it upon himself to set apart Francis Asbury and Thomas Coke, marking the start of Methodism in America.

These attempts to "reform" the Church failed in so far as inner-reform, but succeeded in bringing forth change outside the existing structure, resulting in the formation of various denominations. Along with renewed emphasis on Salvation, these groups strengthened the evangelical stream, but weakened the liturgical-sacramental stream. Wesley was the exception. He was an Anglican and died an Anglican. He encouraged the liturgical pattern for worship although most of his followers in the new world disregarded his admonitions. The Pentecostal emphasis was virtually ignored. The development of the monastic orders, and the abuse of the Papacy, instigated much reaction to the liturgy and sacraments by the reformers and their advocates.

Over the years there have been groups that broke from the Church placing them outside the mainstream of the Christian Church. Some of these groups acted totally independent of other Christian bodies, thus placing themselves apart from any corporate authority. For the first thousand years there was one Church. In the past five hundred years there has emerged over 40,000 different denominations or independent bodies.

In the mid-1800s the Holy Spirit began to be experienced in the Russian Orthodox Church in a similar way the early Church experienced His presence. Church members manifested the *"charismata"* of the Spirit. Prophecy and speaking in tongues quickly brought forth persecution, and many of the Orthodox believers fled to Armenia. They were not any more welcomed in their new land than they had been in Russia. A prophecy was heeded by many of the Armenians, and they fled to the United States about the turn of the century while many others were killed by the Turkish invasion.

At the same time, similar revivals of the Holy Ghost were taking place in Germany, Wales and other parts of Europe. Response was the same as in the Russian Church, culminating in a quasi-official formation of the Pentecostal Church soon after the turn of the century.

In a Kansas town about this same time, a group of Methodists had begun to study the Bible in a home group. They were studying the Acts of the Apostles. When they read of the things that occurred in the first century Church, they asked why were these things not still happening. They began to pray, and this group experienced the same phenomenon we read about in Acts 2, Acts 8, Acts 10, and Acts 19 pertaining to the Holy Spirit. Their "tongue speaking" was not welcomed either. Some of those whose lives had been touched by the Holy Spirit moved to Los Angeles where also the Armenians had retreated. God brought the two groups together at a place located on Azusa Street, and there followed a Holy Ghost revival that lasted for a half dozen years. Out of this event came eventually the Pentecostal churches, forced to separate from the mainline denominations because their experience and fervor were unwelcome, as had occurred in Europe.

In 1955 students at leading universities in the United States stirred reports of tongue speaking, but little credibility was given to it. University students are known to do weird things, and a religious experience was of no consequence any more than eating gold fish or setting a record by seeing how many students can get inside a telephone booth.

But when a few years later mainline denominational leaders began to speak in tongues, prophesy, and conduct healing services, the seriousness of this renewed move of

God began to be considered important. Men such as Father Dennis Bennett of the Episcopal Church, Dr. Brick Bradford of the Presbyterian Church, the Rev. Harold Brown of the United Church of Christ, and Brother Ralph Martin in the Roman Catholic Church provided "respectability" to what had earlier been declared "a phase". The "Charismatic Movement" was born, and hundreds of thousands of Christians in mainline denominations began to experience Pentecost during the period of 1968-1976 in a sweeping move of the Holy Spirit.

There is always a danger associated with the wonders of God. Man is not content with trusting God to weave within ordinary life the mysteries of His Kingdom. With every mighty move of God there has been a time of exuberant and vital response, but subsides when man seeks acceptance and approval from the critics. This involves compromise, and Jesus' message to the Church in Laodicea [Revelation 3: 14-21] clearly states His position regarding churches that fail to take a definite stand. This would also apply to movements. Is it possible that the decline in the numbers who received the Baptism in the Holy Spirit after the mid-seventies could be attributed to an attempt to achieve acceptability with most denominations making a token acceptance?

The Convergence Movement is like an ocean into which flows the three major streams of Christianity - the evangelical, the charismatic/Pentecostal, and the liturgical-sacramental. I am tempted to use the word "catholic" for the latter emphasis, and hesitate because most people associate the word solely with the Roman Church. "Catholic" means universal, one, and adequately describes the Church as the Body of Christ. To use that term is to bridge the chasm caused by denominationalism, and embraces the historical truths that belong to the whole Church. Jesus gave us Sacraments. The writings of the Church Fathers clearly prescribe liturgical practices. This is the beauty of the Church catholic!

The three streams have their origin in Jesus Christ. The early church did not hesitate to declare belief in Jesus as the Son of God, crucified, and raised from the dead, as fundamental for salvation. The early church also realized the need for POWER that comes through the indwelling of the Holy Spirit. This is evidenced by the sending of Peter and John to impart the Holy Spirit to new believers in Samaria [Acts 8: 14-17]. Three Sacraments [Baptism, The Lord's Supper, Unction] are very obvious as having been directed by Jesus, and Holy Orders might be implied in the commission of the Apostles to go forth into the world [Matt 28: 16-20]. Penance gets its name from the assignment given the repentant for purposes of strengthening him against a repeat of the sin, but the word Confession would be more descriptive of this Sacrament, and it is clearly taught by St James [James 5:16]. Confirmation is the Apostolic imparting of the strengthening gifts of the Holy Spirit that follows the outpouring of the Spirit on the Day of Pentecost, and obviously became the norm for the early Church. Holy Matrimony is the only one of the traditional seven Sacraments that is not clearly rooted in Jesus or the first Apostles, unless you want to use Jesus at the Cana wedding.

Nevertheless, these three streams when equally emphasized provide the balance needed for the Church to manifest the Body of Christ in our time. Jesus prayed in John 17: 21 [KJV]: *"That they all may be one; as thou, Father, art in me, and I in thee, that they also may be one in us: that the world may believe that thou hast sent me."*

26

They have always been part of the church, but during certain periods of the church's life, not emphasized or one stream emphasized more over another. The scandal of Christianity is the divisiveness of the Church seen in the more than 40,000 denominations and independent groups today.

The Convergence Movement seeks to restore that balance. This may be God's move to fulfill the prayer of Jesus. The movement is still very new, and like an infant taking his first steps, there will be falls and recoveries in the process of maturing. The Charismatic Episcopal Church is the best evidence of holy men prayerfully seeking and following the move of God as these streams are restored as collectively manifested in One Church.

Church History Timeline Chart
JESUS CHRIST IS LORD!
He starts His Church.....

The history of the church may be best portrayed as one river flowing from its Source, divided into three streams at certain intervals of its flow. As with all rivers flowing towards a common destiny, the streams in Christianity flow toward a common destiny. The ocean of the Christian streams may be called The Convergence Movement. The Charismatic Episcopal Church is one of several expressions of this ocean.

THE THREE STREAMS

The **CHURCH** was **ONE** stream from Jesus – evangelical, Pentecostal, and Sacramental.

DIVERGENCE occurred with division 1054 but still one [*catholic*] in that it remained **Liturgical and Sacramental.**

REFORMATION attempts split the western branch [Roman Catholic] creating the **Evangelical** stream.

PENTECOSTAL RESTORATION began mid-1800s in both streams, and was rejected, creating a third stream.

The three streams [liturgical-sacramental, evangelical, Pentecostal] **converge** into **ONE CONVERGENCE** "ocean", and CEC is one expression of Convergence.

GOVERNED BY BISHOPS

Apostolic Succession is the manner of transferring authority through the laying-on-of-hands to men who are chosen to govern the Church. St Polycarp, the successor of St John the Divine, said Jesus gave specific instructions to St John on how the authority of the Church was to be passed from the first Apostles He had commissioned on to those who would continue authority over the Church. Prior to His Ascension, Jesus gave authority to the first Apostles: *"Jesus came and space unto them, saying, all power is given unto me in heaven and in earth. Go ye therefore, and teach all nations, baptizing them in the name of the Father, and of the Son, and of the Holy Ghost: Teaching them to observe all things whatsoever I have commanded you: and, lo, I am with you always, even unto the end of the world. Amen."* [Mat 28:18-20 KJV]

St John laid hands on St Polycarp and made him Bishop of Smyrna. He laid hands on another and made him a bishop. And the process continued from one to the next unto this day. It is through this process of Consecration that the Holy Spirit is invoked, and a man is made a Bishop. Through the line of succession the Church has its historic roots to Jesus Christ Himself, and with the laying-on-of-hands men are entrusted to perpetuate the Faith in the life and teachings of Jesus Christ and through the Sacraments of the Church. Although in its infancy, the authority is transmitted one-on-one, the church today, desiring to avoid any brokenness in the line, normally would have a minimum of three bishops to lay hands on a new bishop. Historically it is not required.

Since Bishop Randolph Adler was the first Patriarch of the Charismatic Episcopal Church, we shall consider only his consecration and apostolic line. He has been the chief consecrator in most of the consecration of Charismatic Episcopal Church Bishops, and chief consecrator in sufficient number of the first bishops to assure the validity of their line of succession back to the first Apostles and to Jesus Christ Himself.

Austin Randolph Adler was consecrated on June 26, 1992 by Bishop Timothy Michael Barker of the International Free Catholic Communion, whose Syrian line of Succession can be traced through lines of Rome, Canterbury, Constantinople, Utrecht, Chaldea, Assyria, Syria, Armenia, and Albania. A complete treatment of this subject may be read in, "*Apostolic Succession*" by the Rev. Canon Rick E. Hatfield. The evidence compiled by Canon Hatfield's in-depth investigation amounts to more than several reams of paper. Only a small portion of that investigation and tracing of every line that culminated in Bishop Barker is printed in "*Apostolic Succession*". Bishop Adler's Apostolic line was strengthened (the term is *sub conditione)* later through Bishop William Millsaps of the Anglican Province of South Africa, (later Presiding Bishop of the Episcopal Missionary Church in USA) providing a clear Anglican line all the way back to St James the Less recognized as the First Bishop of Jerusalem. His *"sub conditione"* also contains the Protestant Episcopal Church in the United States of America lineage through Bishop James Cortez West of the Reformed Episcopal Church whose line of succession goes back to Bishop John Henry Hopkins of the Protestant Episcopal Church in the United States of America.

Sub conditione is the term used in sacramental theology for strengthening, perfecting or assuring something done that may questionable or uncertain, is made certain by repeating the sacrament. Some people who are unsure they were baptized in infancy may be "re-baptized *sub-conditione*" in which the priest administering the Sacrament of Baptism will say, "if you have not been baptized, I now baptize you in the Name of the Father, and the Son, and the Holy Spirit." Critics have attempted to dismiss the *sub conditione* consecration of Bishop Randolph Adler on the grounds of repetition, yet would not hesitate presenting a questionable candidate for Baptism or Confirmation.

On November 5, 1997 three bishops of the National Catholic Apostolic Church of Brazil [Patriarch Luis Fernando Castillo Mendez, the Primate and Vice-Primate] laid hands on five Charismatic Episcopal Church bishops, including Patriarch Adler, strengthening the Church's Apostolic Succession, and making the International Communion of the Charismatic Episcopal Church's line of Apostolic Succession only one consecration removed from a direct Roman line back to the throne of St. Peter, first Bishop of Rome. Bishop Mendez was consecrated by Bishop Carlos Duarte Costa, formerly the Roman Catholic Diocesan Bishop of Botucatu (San Paolo, Brazil) who established the Catholic Apostolic Church of Brazil when he separated from Rome over the mistreatment of the Brazilian people by the Papal Nuncio. This apostolic line has never been disputed by the Vatican, and totally recognized although the church is not under the Papacy.

Carlos Duarte Costa was ordained a Brazilian Bishop in 1924 in the Roman Catholic Church. He was very outspoken in defending the poor. In 1937 at the insistence of the dictatorial Getulio Vargas regime in Brazil, the Vatican forced Monsignor Costa to retire as Bishop of Botucatu. Nonetheless, he continued in speaking out on behalf of the poor and, in 1944, was even imprisoned for several months because of his opposition to the Brazilian government's protection of Nazis, and the Pope's refusal to speak out against the German war crimes. Finally, in 1945, after protesting the Vatican's having assisted several Nazis find refuge in Brazil he broke with Rome and established the Catholic Apostolic Church of Brazil.

Over the next fifteen years, Monsignor Costa, along with the first two bishops he consecrated (Bishop Salameo Ferraz and Bishop Luis Fernando Castillo-Mendez) helped form in Latin America several other Catholic Apostolic Churches. Salameo Ferraz was born in Sao Paolo Brazil in the latter part of the nineteenth century. He was ordained a Roman Catholic priest in 1935. On August 15, 1945 he left the Roman Catholic Church and was received into the Catholic Apostolic Church of Brazil. He was immediately consecrated coadjutor bishop by Bishop Carlos Duarte Costa. In 1958 Bishop Ferraz, now a married Catholic Apostolic bishop, returned to the Roman Catholic Church under Pope Pius XII. He was never re-consecrated a Bishop by the Roman Catholic Church, not even conditionally (*sub conditione*). By receiving Bishop Ferraz in this manner, the Roman Catholic Church thereby affirmed both *de jure and de facto* that the consecration he received within the Catholic Apostolic Church of Brazil was valid.

Bishop Ferraz was an active speaker in all four sessions of the Vatican Council II, and was named titular bishop of Eleuterna in Crete by Pope John XXIII on May 12, 1963. It was in this capacity that he died in 1969 and buried with full honors accorded a Bishop of the Roman Catholic Church.

Luis Fernando Castillo Mendez was ordained a
Roman Catholic priest in 1944. Like Monsignor Costa, he
was a champion of the poor in Venezuela, and was exiled
for nine months on an island without food or clothing.
Fisherman came to his rescue and eventually he was able to
escape exile, and went to Panama where he was
consecrated a Bishop by Monsignor Costa in 1948. He is
the sole surviving bishop consecrated by Monsignor Costa.
Patriarch Mendez died in October 2009.

All bishops in the Charismatic Episcopal Church
have now had their consecration strengthened by
subsequent laying-on-of-hands, as well as all the clergy
ordained prior to November 5, 1997, conveying through the
laying-on-of-hands, and prayer the strongest line of
Apostolic Succession there possibly can be obtained.
There should be no question of verifiability as to the
Apostolic Succession of Bishops in the Charismatic
Episcopal Church. At this time, unofficially, Roman
Catholic Canon Lawyers say the apostolic line of the
Charismatic Episcopal Church is impeccable. This is the
nearest word to "acceptance and acknowledgement of
validity" we can hope for since the Charismatic Episcopal
Church is not in communion with the Vatican.

It is unfortuante that after the CEC consecration by
Patriarch Mendez, in his deteriorating age he was "used" by
groups seeking Apostolic Succession, and conveyed the
Rebiba line to men who are ordaining people contrary to
Scripture and the catholic faith. This in no way, however,
invalidates the authenticity of our Apostolic Succession.

More than ninety percent of today's Roman
Catholic bishops trace their episcopal lineage back to one
bishop who was consecrated on March 16, 1541. All of the

Charismatic Episcopal Church's bishops trace their lineage to the same bishop, Scipione Rebiba. Prior to Rebiba's consecration there was no dispute, but with the English reformation resulting in the excommunication of the Church in England by the Pope, and the fragmenting of the Church through the Protestant Reformation, lines of apostolic succession since have come into question. It is widely accepted that Bishop Rebiba was consecrated by Gian Pietro Cardinal Carafa who became Pope Paul IV.

The Rebiban Succession

AUSTIN RANDOLPH ADLER was consecrated Bishop for the International Communion of the Charismatic Episcopal Church on November 5, 1997 by Luis Castillo Mendez with Dom Josivaldo Olivera, and Dom Olinto Ferreira Pinto Filho as co- consecrators.

LUIS CASTILLO MENDEZ was consecrated Bishop of the Catholic Apostolic Church Brazil on May 3, 1948 by Carlos Duarte-Costa, Primate and founding bishop of the Catholic Apostolic Church of Brazil.

CARLOS DUARTE-COSTA was consecrated Titular Bishop of Maura and Diocesan Bishop of Botucatu, Sao Paulo, Brazil of t he Roman Catholic Church on December 8, 1924 by Sebastiao Leme de Silveira Cintra, Titular Bishop of Orthosia who was also later Cardinal and Archbishop of Rio de Janeiro; assisted by Dom Alberto Jose Goncalves and Dom Beneditio Paulo Alves de Souza. Duart-Costa established the Catholic Apostolic Church of Brazil July 6, 1945 subsequent to his expulsion from the Roman Catholic Church by Pope Pius XII.

SEBASTIAO LEME DE SILVEIRA CINTRA was consecrated Titular Bishop of Orthosia on June 4, 1911 by Joaquin de Alburquerque-Calvacanti, Bishop of Goia, and was later named Cardinal and Archbishop of Rio de Janeiro.

JOAQUIN DE ALBURQUERQUE-CALVACANTI was consecrated Bishop of Goia on October 26, 1890 by Mariano Rampolla Marchese del Tindaro, Titular Archbishop of Heraclea; and was later named Cardinal in 1905.

MARIANO RAMPOLLA MARCHESE DEL TINDARO was consecrated Titular Archbishop of Heraclea on December 8, 1882 by Edward Howard, Titular Archbishop of Neocaesarea and Auxilary Bishop of Frascati; and later named Cardinal in 1887.

EDWARD HOWARD was consecrated Titular Archbishop of Neocaesarea and Auxiliary Bishop of Frascati on June 30, 1872 by Cardinal Charles Sacconi, Titular Archbishop of Nicaea assisted by Archbishops Salvator Nobili Vitelleschi and Franciscus Xaverius Fredericus de Merode; and was later named Cardinal.

CHARLES SACCONI was consecrated Titular Archbishop of Nicaea on June 8, 181 **by** James Phillip Fransoni, Archbishop of Nazianzus; and was later named Cardinal.

JAMES PHILLIP FRANSONI was consecrated Titular Archbishop of Nazianzus on December 8, 1822 by Peter Francis Galetti, Titular Archbishop of Damascus, assisted by Patriarch Joseph Valerga and Bishop Rudensindus Salvado; and was later named Cardinal.

PETER FRANCIS GALETTI was consecrated Titular Archbishop of Damascus on September 12, 1819 by Alexander Matthaeus, Archbishop of Ferrara, assisted by Archbishops Joannes Franciscus Falzacappa and Josephus delia Porta Rondlana; and in 1803 was named Cardinal.

ALEXANDER MATTHAEUS was consecrated Archbishop of Ferrara on February 23, 1777 by Bernadinus Giraud, Titular Archbishop of Damascus, assisted by Bishops Geraldus Macloti and Franciscus Albertini; and in 1779 was named Cardinal.

BERNADINUS GIRAUD was consecrated Titular Archbishop of Damascus on April 26, 1767 by Carlo Rezzonico, Cardinal Bishop of Padova, assisted by Archbishop Marcus Antionius Conti and Bishop Losefus Maria Carafa.

CARLO della Torre REZZONICO, Cardinal Bishop of Padova; the future Pope Clement XIII was consecrated March 19, 1743 in the Basilica of the Twelve Holy Apostles, Rome, by His Holiness Pope Benedict XIV, assisted by Giuseppe Cardinal Accoramboni, Bishop of Frascati and Antonio Saverio Cardinal Gentili.

PROSPERO LAMBERTINI, Titular Archbishop of Theodosia, the future Pope Benedict XIV was consecrated July 16, 1724 in the Pauline Chapel of the Apostolic Palace of the Quirinal, Rome, by His Holiness Pope Benedict XIII, assisted by Giovanni Francesco Nicolai, O.F.M.Ref., Titular Archbishop of Myra and Nicola Maria Lercari, Titular Archbishop of Nazianzus. **Prospero Lorenzo Lambertini and those previous to him, are in the Episcopal Lineage of His Holiness, John Paul II - Karl Wojtyla.**

VICENZO MARIA ORSINI, O.P., Cardinal Archbishop of Manfredonia, the future Pope Benedict XII was consecrated February 3, 1675 in the Church of SS Dominco e Sisto, Rome, by Paluzzo (Paluzzo degli Albertoni) Cardinal Altieri, Prefect of the Sacred Congregation de Propaganda Fide, assisted by Stefano Brancaccio, Archbishop-Bishop of Viterbo e Tuscania and Costanzo Zani, O.S.B., Bishop of Imola.

PALUZZO (PALUZZI degli ALBERTONI) ALTIERI, Cardinal Bishop of Bontifiascone e Corneto was consecrated May 2, 1666 in the Church of San Silvestro in Capite, Rome, by Ulderico Cardinal Carpegna, assisted by Stafano Ugolini, Titular Archbishop of Corinth and Giovanni Tommaso Pinelli, Bishop of Albenga.

ULDERICO CARPEGNA, Bishop of Gubbio was consecrated October 7, 1630 in the Pauline Chapel of the Apostolic Palace of the Quirinal, Rome, By Luigi Cardinal Caetani, assisted by Antonio Ricciulli, Bishop emeritus of Belcastro and Vicegerent of Rome, and Benedetto Landi, Bishop of Fossombrone.

LUIGI CAETANI, Titulare Patriarch of Antioc was consecrated June 12, 1622 in the Basilica of Santa Maria Maggiore, by Lodovico Cardinal Ludovisi, Archbishop of Bologna, assisted by Galeazzo Sanvitale, Archbishop emeritus of Bari and Vulpiano Volpi, Archbishop emeritus of Chieti.

LODOVICO LUDOVISI, Cardinal Archbishop of Bologna was consecrated May 2, 1621 in the private chapel of his consecrator, near Saint Peter's Basilica, Rome, by Galeazzo Sanvitale, Archbishop emeritus of Bari and Prefect of the Apostolic Palace, assisted by Cosmo de

Torres, Titular Archbishop of Hadrianopolis and Ottavio Ridolfi, Bishop of Ariano.

GALEAZZO SANVITALE, Archbishop of Bari was consecrated April 4, 1604 in the chapel of the Apostolic Sacristy, Rome, by Girolamo Cardinal Bernerio, O.P., Bishop of Albano, assisted by Claudio Rangoni, Bishop of Piacenza and Giovanni Ambrogio Caccia, Bishop of Castro di Toscana.

GIROLAMO BERNERIO, O.P. Bishop of Ascoli Piceno was consecrated September 7, 1586 in the Basikca of the Twelve Holy Apostles, Rome, by Giulio Antonio Cardinal Santoro, assisted by Giulio Masetti, Bishop of Reggio Emilia and Ottaviano Patrvicini, Bishop of Alexandria.

GIULIO ANTONIO SANTORO, Archbishop of Santa Severina was consecrated March 12, 1566 in the Pauline Chapel of the Vatican Apostolic Palace by Scipione Cardinal Rebiba, Titular Patriarch of Constantinople, assisted by Annibale Caracciolo, Bishop of Isola and Giacomo de Giacomelli, Bishop emeritus of Belcastro.

SCIPIONE REBIBA, Titular Bishop of Amicle and Auxiliary Bishop of Chieti, Elected Titular Bishop of Amicle and Auxilary to Gian Pietro Cardinal Carafa, Archbishop of Chiete, Titular Patriarch of Constantinople, was consecrated on March 16, 1541 by Gian Pietro Cardinal Carafa who became Pope Paul IV.

Scipione Cardinal Rebiba is the source point for the Episcopal lineage of a vast majority of bishops with roots in the Roman Catholic lineage. The Episcopal lineage is important to the Church because it is one viable and visible link for the contemporary church to the founding Apostles and Jesus Christ himself. In Matthew 28:18-20, commonly called the Apostolic Commission, Jesus states four important facts. The Apostles were to (1) Make Disciples, (2) Baptize, (3) and Teach. The fourth was Jesus' promise to always be with them. The Bishop is an icon of Jesus Christ's authority in His Church, and authentic Apostolic Succession gives assurance to believers of Jesus' Headship over the Church. The Apostolic Succession is traced via different consecration lines within the Roman Catholic, Orthodox and Anglican communions. The lineage from Scipione Cardinal Rebiba to the present day is important to be noted because it was after the time of the Rebiba Succession that the Church in England separated from the Roman Catholic Church, and many Roman Catholic Bishops trace their lineage through Rebiba.

Patriarch Luis Edwardo Fernando Castillo-Mendez

The word "episcopal" signifies a Church that is governed by Bishops. It comes from the Greek *"episcopos"* used by St. Paul in his pastoral epistles to Timothy and

Titus. We are indebted to St. Paul for the information concerning the order of ministry in the early Church.

The uniqueness of the Charismatic Episcopal Church is in its government. Unlike any other denomination, the Charismatic Episcopal Church governs throughout the Church by consensus. The New Testament teaches the priesthood of believers through the operation of the gifts and ministry of the Holy Spirit, but not in government. The Church is a Theocratic organism, not a democratic organization. God's Voice is one! Consensus government is very different from a majority rule process. By consensus decisions are reached through prayer depending upon the leading of the Holy Spirit. Consensus is derived at, not through a voting procedure, but through a relational process. This form of government is at every level of the church's life from the local parish all the way up to the Patriarch's Council, demanding a relationship of trust. Westerners have difficulty with this concept. Easterners, especially Asians, understand it. The process cannot adequately be explained; it just happens! Working with Asians, I have watched a group of leaders come together and discuss everything under the sun, perhaps over a meal. The frustration to a westerner is the apparent lack of agenda. Westerners have issues and seek to make concrete decisions on each issue at hand. Easterners seek to build a relationship, a mutual trust, an underlying understanding. Sometime the issue may never be the center of the conversation, but when the relationship is cemented, the issue is likewise cemented. It works.

I had an occasion to meet Randolph Alder for breakfast. I had carefully prepared an agenda of items I wished to discuss with him. Strangely enough, in the two hours we were together, I never mentioned a single item on my agenda list, however, when we parted, all the things I wanted discussed were resolved. In the building of a relationship of understanding, the issues were settled.

In the Charismatic Episcopal Church there is no Vestry, Session or Administrative Board. At the local parish level the priest chooses a council of men. They meet regularly to pray about those matters pertaining to the life of the Church. While the Priest has the ultimate word, he would be unwise to act apart from the advice of his council. The concept of the Council is to discern the Voice of God, and when properly obeyed, the process will result in a clear Unity in the Holy Spirit. Consensus requires respect for authority, and submission to those whom God has placed in position of spiritual leadership over His Church. The greatest opposition from some congregational ruled churches against entering the Charismatic Episcopal Church is the surrender of control. In every respect to the government and operation of the local church, the priest is in charge. His authority as spiritual leader [Father] of his congregation is accepted. He is expected to prayerful seek the Holy Spirit in every phase of the church's life, and his discernment, if truly of God, is confirmed by his Council.

At the Diocesan level the Council is composed of the Bishop and clergy. At the National Church level there is the House of Bishops, and on the International level the Patriarch along with the other Archbishops seek consensus of what the Holy Spirit leads the church to do.

The primary governing body of the Church is the House of Bishops. Presently they meet twice a year. The Patriarch's Council that sets the agenda for the House of Bishops precedes each meeting. As the Patriarch's Council prays and discerns the Mind of God, they come to a decision as to what is to be considered by the Bishops who normally meet immediately upon the close of the Patriarch's Council. His Council is composed of the Archbishops and others whom the Patriarch selects. Only the House of Bishops speaks officially for the Church in matters of doctrine and discipline.

CHARISMATIC EPISCOPAL CHURCH EPISCOPATE
Active and Retired Bishops of October 2011
In the Order of their Consecration

FIRST PATRIARCH AUSTIN RANDOLPH ADLER
Retired

Delmar Robinson - Emeritus
Loren Thomas Hines – Primate of Asia
Douglas Kessler – General Secretary and Western Province USA
Jose Elmer Medrano Belmonte – Europe

John Holloway – Retired
Charles "Chuck" Jones – Archbishop of Southeast Province
USA
Benson Odinga O'Otieno - Kenya - Deceased
Bernard Njoroge Kariuki - Kenya
Raymundo D. Abogatal, Jr. - Philippines
Ricardo Alcarez – Philippines
Lowell Eugene Lilly, Jr. – Philippines
CRAIG W. BATES - Current Patriarch; Primate of USA; Bishop of Northeast Province

The Most Reverend Craig W. Bates, Patriarch

Joseph Mahon – Retired
Paulino Villavicencio – Philippines
Daniel Kimwele – Kenya
Enoch Sasaka – Kenya – Retired
Frank J. Costantino – St Dismas Society - Deceased

Michael Davidson – Central USA
Prakash Yuhanna - Pakistan
Moses Meeli Ngusa – Kenya
Hannington Bahemuka – Uganda
Bernard Afwanda Obora – Kenya
Bernard Matolo – Kenya
Francis Gogo – Uganda
Samuel Kamanya Lubogo - Uganda
Felicismo Cordero – Spain
Peter Zedekiah Otsuhah Chunge – Kenya
Philip Edward Phlegar Weeks – Retired
[Bishop Weeks was Supervising Bishop of Rwanda,
Tanzania, and Burundi]
Joshua Ayoo Koyo – Kenya
Paulo Ruiz Garcia – Primate of Brazil
Emmanuel Ngirumpatse – Rwanda
Prudence Ngarambe – Retired
Charles Sekelwa – Tanzania
Jothan Kabonabe Tibafa – DR Congo
Tom Nak Kokanyi – Sudan
Husto Ntugnwwa Muhereza – Uganda
David Simpson – Florida Diocese USA
Nitonde Dieudonne – Burundi
Nestor Misigaro – Burundi
Katarama Kizungu Sylvain – DR Congo
Alzeandre Barbosa Monteiro Ximenes – Brazil
Frederico Carreiro Rego Bastos – Brazil
Adonias Ramos de Sousa – Brazil
W. David Epps – Mid-South Diocese USA
Solomon Madara Kadiri – Kenya
Gregory Ortiz – Auxiliary Northeast Province
Andre Novas - Brazil
Tobias Onyango Opondo – Kenya
Elias Ntoipo – Kenya
Jackson Ara Luhusa Madulesi – Tanzania

Japheth Iraka –Uganda
Jimmy barmuke Ruskoah – Uganda
Eliasiba Eoja Bute – Sudan
Jacques Muhindo Niravaheren – Uganda
Frederic Lunkomo Bushiri – DR Congo
Ariel Santos – Philippines

**Primate Loren Thomas Hines at the altar of Cathedral
of the King, Manila**

CONVERGENCE WORSHIP

"Non nobis, Domine, sed nomini tuo da gloriam!" This is the theme song of the Charismatic Episcopal Church. "Not to us, O Lord, not to us, but to your Name be the glory...." Psalm 115.1. NIV. It expresses who we are, and manifested in our worship.

Renewal in many mainline churches since the early 1970s has been expressed through traditional worship on Sunday morning, and charismatic expressions coupled with informal worship at some other stated time. We believe it is unnecessary for people to go to Church on Sunday morning to receive the Body and Blood of Jesus, and then go at another time for Prayer and Praise. Worship is the offering of our best in praise to the glory of God who has created us for the purpose of enjoying Him, and our worship is to express both our enjoyment of God and our commitment to Him for our life.

In Charismatic Episcopal Churches you discover a vibrancy of worship; the expectancy that God will visit His people and equip them for the living of these days. Our worship is expected to encompass every way in which we can glorify God. Upon attending a service of convergence worship one person remarked, "they prayed expecting God to attend their Service; and He did!" Convergence worship accepts the Psalmist as knowledgeable when he said, "God inhabits the praises of His people" [Psalm 22:3]. In convergence worship we heed the instruction of St Paul to permit all things that are decent be done in orderliness. [1 Corinthians 14:40]

You will find congregational singing, using a combination of traditional hymns of the Church mixed with more contemporary songs, gospel tunes, and spiritual singing. In First Corinthians [14:15] St Paul says he utilizes every form of verbal expression to pray and worship God. With the lively singing there will be times when the hands are utilized in clapping, and some people may find movement in their feet as they keep time with the music. Some may jump! There is much praise but there are also the solemn moments in song and worship.

In many of our churches, young people have been trained to express praise in worship through liturgical dance. This is not for purposes of entertaining the congregation. It is to enhance the worship in song, and to create within the worshipers the sense of awe and wonderment before a God who has invited us to come before His Mercy Seat. We do not presume we sit at His feet only to receive; we approach His Throne in adoration. The expressions of the liturgical dancers assist us to realize what God has invited us to receive, and instills within us the humility necessary to come before the Lord of Hosts.

Worship in the Charismatic Episcopal Church is a participatory act. In order for us to receive all that God desires to give, we must first be willing to give of ourselves. This requires our participation, and liturgy is the best form by which to enable this to happen. Some people object to liturgy without understanding its purpose. Liturgy is the "work of the people". The worship leader is just that - the worship leader. The people bring their sacrifice of praise and thanksgiving. Every church has some form of liturgy or ritual. I recall one evangelical church in the Philippines where I was so impressed with their style of worship the first time I attended. They sang praise songs because the scripture says, "God inhabits the praises of His people". After some time of praising, their mood shifted to more solemn worship type songs. I thought, "yes, praise gets God's presence, and when He arrives, we worship Him." I was blessed with this wonderful pattern of worship. I returned to this church at a later date, and they followed exactly the same form - four songs of praise, often repetitive; three songs of worship followed by singing in the Spirit, the bidding of a "clap offering to the Lord'" and the invitation to "be seated in the presence of the Lord". It was RITUAL! Every time the same form or pattern regardless who was the worship leader. This church would have strongly rejected liturgical worship, yet they had their own form of liturgy or ritual.

In some places a phrase "God is good'" said by the leader, with the people responding "all the time"; then reversed "all the time'" and the response "God is good" has caught on and spread. That is ritual. It is as much ritual as any order of worship or any liturgical pattern.

Liturgy gives us substance to our worship. It not only provides us a pattern for orderly worship, but through the prayers, scripture readings, songs, and finally receiving the Body and Blood of Jesus, we are connected with the Apostles and Prophets of old as well as the angels and archangels and the whole company of Heaven. We do not propose to depend upon our human abilities to devise the perfect form for worshiping God, nor trust solely in the leadership of one man to direct us to the Throne room. Through ancient formulas, prayers, litanies, hymns, and rituals, we have the benefit of saints from old who have tarried before God much longer than we have, and through their contribution we are brought into oneness with the saints of the first century church, and the hosts that have gone before us. The words of the Sanctus take on added meaning when we understand that through liturgy we indeed join with "angels and archangels, and all the company of heaven" when we worship. I much prefer the leadership provided in liturgical form to the leadership of one man who orchestrates worship according to his own whelms.

Liturgy without the Holy Spirit is dead. This has been the experience of many people who have been exposed to mumble words without expression or life. So-called charismatic worship when contrived can be equally spiritless. Nothing is more joyous than spontaneous response to the move of the Holy Spirit, and nothing more discouraging than a contrived response motivated by an individual leader. Perhaps this bad experience is what motivates objectors to oppose liturgy. The charismatic expression is necessary for liturgy to be alive and meaningful. The danger always lurks around the corner when the people become intent on "perfecting" their liturgical styles, or priests get into "priest-craft" as they go mechanically through form without substance. The substance must be the Holy Spirit giving life not only to the people using the liturgical form, but also giving meaning to the words in the form itself. The Holy Spirit brings alive the words in the liturgy as the people worship in expectancy of the awareness of God's presence. Jesus said "God is spirit, and his worshipers must worship in spirit and in truth," [John 4:24 NIV], and without the Holy Spirit the danger is for the liturgy to be without meaning.

There are places in the liturgy where the manifestations of the Holy Spirit can be operative and maintain the decorum and order of the worship. Some places where singing in tongues or opportunities for a prophetic word to be spoken would be immediately following the Gloria in excelsis, during the season of worship, and at the time of worship immediately following Communion. When the people are made aware that these are proper times for manifestations of spiritual gifts, they will be prepared to respond as the Holy Spirit moves. There is nothing wrong with prescribing certain places where spiritual manifestations may occur. God is a God of order rather than confusion, and the Holy Spirit will be subject to that which is proper in giving praise to God.

Preachers must never forget that there are times when their evangelical message invites a response. I recall one Episcopal Church bishop many years ago, tell how in his younger days he was chastised by a parishioner for failing to give the people the opportunity to respond when he preached evangelical sermons. After this chastisement, he made it a practice always to give people opportunity to respond to the Gospel invitation whether it was by the raising of a hand, standing, or remaining in silence during a time of prayer. One Charismatic Episcopal Church where I have frequented has not forgotten the evangelical emphasis in Convergence Worship. Following every sermon, an invitation to receive Jesus is offered to the congregation. They often have strangers and visitors in their worship, and the opportunity to pray with one who wishes to invite Jesus into their life is provided. The invitation is very simply put: - "If you have never received Jesus as your Savior, I would consider it a privilege to pray with you this morning".

To be true Convergence Worship, there must be the balance of the evangelical, the charismatic, as well as the richness of the liturgy. When evangelical churches adopt liturgy, they must never give up their evangelical zeal lest the liturgy becomes dead. When charismatic churches adopt liturgy, they must never give up their charismatic attitude lest the liturgy becomes dead. The Patriarch enthusiastically encourages manifestations of the Holy Spirit be expressed during corporate worship. Our message calls people to a relationship with God through Jesus Christ's redemption. Our empowerment for living the Christian life and walking the Christian walk comes through the indwelling of the Holy Spirit. We are not giving up anything; we are embracing a richness of the real inheritance God has provided. This is equally true of liturgical churches that embrace Convergence Worship. They must find the evangelical zeal and be re-kindled with the fires of Pentecost.

The prescribe order of liturgy will be determined by the Bishop. Some Bishops are permitting the choice between the older forms of the Book of Common Prayer as well as more recent versions, the Anglican Missal, and the Roman Catholic Missal. The Charismatic Episcopal Church is in the process of developing our own Book of Common Prayer.

In many of our churches the Order for Morning and Evening Prayer are recited daily. The main service of worship remains the Eucharist, a time when the people of God sit at Table with the Lord, and receive His renewing life. The clergy are personally encouraged and expected to recite the Daily Offices, making a symbolic circle of the earth with the same scriptures daily read and the prayers offered.

We have found that even those who are very familiar with Liturgy often fail to understand what is happening in liturgical worship. Those who for the first time are experiencing Liturgy may find it very foreign. The

Instructive Eucharist that follows is one form that can be used to explain to the people the full meaning and understanding of the Liturgy. The order of service may vary according to the practice of the local church. We encourage priests to periodically offer this teaching to their congregations. We have found that when people clearly understand each aspect and purpose of liturgy, they have a greater appreciation for liturgical order. When we had an instructive Eucharist with the church leadership in Kenya, all of the men said it was their first time to really understand the Eucharist. They were former Anglican priests. A charismatic pastor in the Philippines, after participating in an instructive Eucharist, remarked, "our charismatic communion is not enough".

There are variations of the following instructive Eucharist prepared by others in the Charismatic Episcopal Church.

An Invitation To Living Worship
The Convergence Movement
International Communion of the
Charismatic Episcopal Church

[*The following introduction is read before the Prelude begins. It is preferable that the narrator is positioned where only his/her voice is heard and the narrator not seen.*]

God has a wonderful purpose for the Church of Jesus Christ. His desire is for His Church to consistently demonstrate His Glory on earth. Set in the midst of a changing and unstable world, the church is designed to set the course for society. If the church is to function in the totality of God's plan, it is necessary for her to look back and see the things which have made her strong and stable, especially during the darkest moments of history. For many modern-day Christians, there is a vacuum between the early church and its contemporary counterpart. This has made many of us unstable, without identification, a body disconnected from its historic roots. This straying away from the identity of being God's "called out ones" [*ecclesia*] has made many Christians today grope with their reason for existence.

The Convergence Movement seeks to restore the church of our Lord in its totality. It is for this reason that many in the evangelical and charismatic streams have embarked upon a journey to the ancient faith; to discover how the first apostles approached faith, worship and practice and how they governed and gave godly leadership to the church.

Recapturing things from the past does not mean however, that we throw away everything that has been

54

believed and practiced. On the contrary, everything that is learned about the early church serves as a fitting complement to existing understanding of the Holy Scriptures. This blending of the old and new is a timely move to maintain a truly God-centered worship and life style.

Gradually it is discovered that we are not alone; that churches throughout the world are being drawn toward the same direction as the evangelical, charismatic and liturgical-sacramental streams of church heritage merge in a Convergence Movement.

One of the first discoveries is the way we worship. This form of worship is not without basis. The early church being of Jewish origin, worshiped in a similar manner. It was rooted in the celebration of the Christian event – Jesus' death and resurrection. It was God-centered, not man-centered.

The order of worship is called Liturgy from the Greek word meaning "work of the people". It is our work to offer ourselves as a sacrificial offering, made possible and acceptable by virtue of the one offering, the sacrifice of Jesus Christ our Lord. It is done in a corporate assembly with one voice and heart and thus re-enforce our unity and agreement. It proclaims Christ through the Word. Worship finds its height at the Table of the Lord, called communion, where we, as one body, share in the covenant meal which our Lord shared with His disciples and which He shares with us who approach His table in faith.

The Liturgy of the Eucharist is best understood as a journey or procession. It is the journey of the Church into the dimension of the Kingdom. In order to fulfill this journey, we must of necessity be one with the Body of Christ. We encourage you to participate with us as we adore our King. Only then will you appreciate the beauty of Liturgy. Allow the Holy Spirit to unfold to you the surpassing greatness of His grace and ability from the beginning to the end. Open yourself to let His Divine Power bring healing and restoration to your spirit, soul and body. Worship, if taken with the right attitude, shapes the way we live daily. Glorification of God is the primary intention, joined with the bestowal of redeeming grace upon men.

Finally, as to the sacraments, their primary purpose is man's participation in Divine Life. Our partaking of the Body of Christ and His Blood feeds us with Divine provision - Eternal Life. We go forth and live the life He has given us, so that in turn, we can bring glory to His Name. We invite you to a living worship of God.
Reader will pause!

AN INSTRUCTIVE EUCHARIST!

[Each part is first read and then done, pausing after that part of the Liturgy is done, waiting for the next segment to be narrated.]

THE PRELUDE
We are encouraged by the music to set ourselves aside from the cares and burdens of this world and to get a glimpse of the throne room of our God.   ***Reader will stop for Prelude!***

THE PROCESSIONAL

Our journey begins with the entrance of the church into the Lord's presence. The clergy and others who will function at the altar enter following the Cross, a bold proclamation of our faith, and led by the Word of God showing that the church is not led by personalities but by the Cross and the Word. When Incense is used, it represents the prayers of the people ascending to the throne room making way for those who will follow. The torches show the light that our faith brings into the darkness. As the procession reaches the altar, the clergy pause but do not enter until each one is prepared to follow. As we would not meet royalty or dignitaries without proper preparation, we should not think we could just barge into the presence of the Lord without acknowledging His greatness and our dependence upon Him.   ***Processional Hymn!***

THE ACCLAMATION

The Celebrant leads the Church to express its purpose and destiny, and acknowledge God for His faithfulness. "Blessed be God..." To bless is to accept the love of the Father and respond to it by our thanksgiving. We bless His Kingdom and the eternal scope of this Kingdom. Our goals are set. ***Acclamation Recited!***

THE COLLECT FOR PURITY

Can we reach such an awesome goal? The Celebrant prays and asks God to help us. "Cleanse our hearts and inspire us by the Holy Spirit that we can love You perfectly and magnify You and Your name". With our prayer to God for help now uttered, we proceed with fuller understanding of our task ahead.   ***Collect prayed!***

THE SUMMARY OF THE LAW and Kyrie [Trisagion]
We are reminded of the Jewish Shema ["the Lord Thy God is One Lord"] in Jesus' Summary of the Law, citing how we are to love the Lord our God and our neighbor. The Deacon [*if there is one*] steps forth and declares aloud this Command of the Lord. Recognizing that we cannot fulfill this on our own, we ask God for mercy in either the Kyrie or Trisagion. The church now taking the step of faith enters into the mercy and grace of God.
Summary & Kyrie!

===

[*At certain seasons of the church year, and in some churches, the Penitential Order will come here rather than after the Prayers of the People. If the Penitential Order comes after the Prayers of the People, transfer this paragraph to that position.*)

CONFESSION OF SINS and ABSOLUTION
Realizing our own lack, we specifically confess our sins that we may have cleansing to enter the Holy of Holies. Confession is our means of receiving the forgiveness of our Lord. The Bible tells us to confess our sins and receive healing. It is a constant awareness of our dependence upon Jesus our Lord. Our confession is an agreement with God that we have sinned and need His mercy if we are to enter His Presence. In commissioning the first apostles, Jesus said, "those whose sins you forgive, they shall be forgiven". Our Lord promises forgiveness of sins to the repentant and the Celebrant declares that forgiveness in the Name of Jesus Christ. ***Confession!***
===

58

GLORY TO GOD

We now lift our voices in proclaiming the Glory due His Name. Our attention is no longer focused on our weakness but upon His love and grace toward us His People. Therefore, we rejoice!

Gloria in excelsis! Or other hymn of praise!

COLLECT of the DAY

With Praise on our lips, faith and a high level of confidence, the Celebrant turns and encourages the people: "The Lord be with you". We are assured that we are not alone, but the Lord is with us. The Church responds by expressing their faith in God and their willingness to follow. They tell the Celebrant "lead on and we will follow you as you lead us to the Lord" by saying, "and also with your spirit".

The Celebrant leads the prayer as he prays the Collect of the Day, a special prayer that draws our thoughts to the central theme of the day. It sets the course and direction for our encounter with the Almighty.

[PAUSE: for the Collect of Day to be prayed]

At the conclusion of the prayer, the first exciting move is made. We are now ready to enter the Sanctuary of the Lord. Up until now we have been in the outer court but now with excitement in our hearts, faith in our Almighty God and enabled by His Grace, we take the first step of faith to enter in. The Celebrant and the altar ministers are seated around the Altar to listen to the lessons that we may know God's ways more intently. Notice how reverently we have approached this moment to sit at His feet and listen to Him teach us. We have given Him Glory due His Name. We have not "barged in", but with love and admiration, we have acknowledged our weakness and His greatness, and proclaimed our love for Him.   *Short pause!*

THE FIRST LESSON

First, a reading from the Old Testament is heard, often preparing our hearts for the fulfillment of God's Divine purpose as brought forth in Jesus Christ our Lord. We respond with a portion from the Book of Psalms - the Jewish hymnal. Following each reading we are reminded that we have heard the Word of the Lord and respond with thanks. We sit quietly for a brief time to ponder the Word of God.   *OT lesson and Psalm!*

A SEASON OF WORSHIP

A time of spontaneous praise and worship through music and/or liturgical dance is interwoven between the readings as part of our response to God's grace in His Word. We are encouraged to present a corporate response to God by putting our love into song and worship. *Worship in the Spirit!*

THE SECOND LESSON

A second reading, this time from the New Testament as we hear about what God did in the early Church, and our desire is heightened that God will do again in His Church the mighty deeds of old.   *NT lesson!*

THE GRADUAL

At last we are ready to hear directly from our Lord in the Gospel. The Gospel is taken in procession into the midst of the people as we sing a song of praise for the illumination of the Words of Eternal Life. The people face the Cross. The torches direct all attention to the Gospel as it gains a prominent place in our hearts.
        Procession of the Gospel!

THE HOMILY

The Celebrant or other designated person expounds on the message of the Lord to us for the day. We learn how we can be the people of God and His witnesses in the world today. *Sermon!*

THE NICENE CREED

Our forefathers set a standard for us so we could not be easily led astray. The Word given must be measured by that standard. Since the year 325 A.D. the Nicene Creed has provided us a standard by which we can judge the word spoken. We declare these words as our affirmation of faith in the Word of God. *The Creed!*

THE PRAYERS OF THE PEOPLE

Having recognized and accepted our place in the Kingdom, we now intercede for the Church and the world. The Church is God's kingdom of a priesthood of believers, sharing the priestly ministry of Jesus our High Priest as we lift the needs of the people before the Throne of Grace. We do not come into His presence just for our own wants and needs; instead, we realize what He has done for us so we can pray for the Church and the World. In many places Incense will dramatize the ascending prayers of the people. As the smoke goes up, so our prayers are received in the throne room of heaven. *The Prayers!*

==

When the Penitential Order is not at the start of the Liturgy, the Confession and Absolution comes here

==

THE PEACE

Having entered the throne room of God through our prayers and intercessions, we are assured that we need not be anxious or fearful. As we are assured that God is at peace with us, we are reminded we must also be at peace with each other. We cannot come to the Table of the Lord with hate or un-forgiveness in our heart. We further our preparation of fellowship with the Lord by sharing the peace of God with others.   *The Liturgical Peace!*

THE OFFERTORY
The next part of our journey to the Kingdom, the Table of the Lord, is our offering. From of old, the pattern has been set that offerings are to be made to the Lord. We bring Him our tithes and offerings, our special thanksgivings, the bread and wine that He may use them for our betterment. What we give to Him, He can then change and when they come back to us they will be more effective. As the offerings are being gathered, the Deacon sets the Table for the Feast. The Celebrant puts on a chasuble, a garment that symbolizes the new robe of the Resurrected Christ.   *Tithes, Offerings, and Special Thanksgivings!*

THE DOXOLOGY
The doxology is recognition of our dependence upon the Almighty. It is an expression of thanksgiving in song to God who provides abundantly for His own - all things are from God. The Altar, the gifts and the givers may be blessed with the incense, a symbol of purifying and cleansing. The Celebrant washes his hands, symbolic of the final steps of cleansing before handling the sacrament, recognition, and the awareness of our need of Jesus and His purification.   *Presentation and Doxology!*

THE GREAT THANKSGIVING
The Celebrant makes the final invitation and the people prepare themselves with excitement as they are

called into the Throne Room of the Almighty. Reminding the people that the Lord is with them, the Celebrant invites them to "lift up your hearts". Realizing what Jesus is about to give us we give thanks and praise as we approach His table for His Feeding. We are nearing the highest point of our journey, the Eucharist - the Great Thanksgiving.

We sing "Holy, Holy, Holy" joining our voices with the angels and archangels and all the company of heaven. One cannot achieve a more majestic moment in our journey. Earth and heaven unite in praise to the Lamb. The Sanctus is recognition of where we are and who is with us. We glorify the Lamb, for it has been His sacrifice given in our place that has freed us from our sin, and has broken the hold of darkness over us.

[*The Sursum Corda, Preface and Sanctus are recited, followed with the Prayer of Consecration up to the "Mystery of Faith"*]

==

THE MYSTERY OF FAITH [*Depending upon the Prayer of Consecration used, a proclamation of our faith may or may not be raised*]

We raise our voices to rejoice in the complete plan of God. We remember that through His death our sins are atoned for, and by His resurrection we are assured of a new body when He comes again. We set our eyes toward the day when the Church will be spotless, having put on the garments provided by Jesus Christ who comes for His Bride. *Mystery Proclaimed!*
==

[*The Prayer of Consecration continues up to the Invitation to the people to receive*]

HOLY COMMUNION

The breaking of bread signifies the act of true love: self-giving. He freely gave His life for us and now gives His life to us. The whole existence and reason for the church and our salvation is tied to this fact of communion - our communion with God and with our brothers in the faith. We go forward to receive the bread and wine as our response to the Lord's invitation to come to His table. We see not ordinary bread and wine, but bread and wine offered to God that now become for us the true bread that has come down from heaven, and the true drink that is poured out for us - the Body and the Blood of Jesus.
Distribution of Sacrament!

WORSHIP AT THE EUCHARIST

Expression of the praise of our hearts is now seen as the people thank God for such a blessing experienced in the Feast. There also may be "manifestations" of the Spirit in operation at this time. *Worship!*

PRAYER AFTER COMMUNION

A final prayer of Thanksgiving is offered for the great joy of feasting with our Lord and we ask Him to strengthen us as we go out into the world to do His will. *Closing Thanksgiving!*

BLESSING AND DISMISSAL

The Celebrant blesses the people, and the Deacon challenges us to go out into the world and live out our Christianity in the darkness as a light shining. The lights on the Altar are extinguished because now the Light is in each of us. Our agreement to all that has been done and said is "AMEN". It is not a sign of being finished; it is an agreement that we have been on a journey to the Kingdom; we have tasted of the Lord and He is good. Man cannot attain sanctification without adoring God, without loving Christ and bending our knee before Him. Our whole life's work is to glorify God. This can be done only when our values are centered on Him. Liturgy has taught us values and priorities. It sets order for our lives, making us more sensitive to the work of God around us and responsive to the Voice of God in our everyday life.

We came out from the world of confusion; we have journeyed into the Kingdom of God; we have feasted with Him at His Table, and now filled with His living Presence, we go forth into the world. We have been changed by His marvelous grace. Now through us He wants to change the world. ***Blessing, Recessional Hymn, Dismissal, Postlude***

American House of Bishops - 2010

LANGUAGE & CULTURE

As we travel in the ministry, there are three young ladies who accompany us. Two are always with us, and the third waits eagerly for an invitation to join in. She must wait outside for the invitation, but the others are always with us in the room where we meet. Please spare judgment until you meet our ladies, for you may be surprised to learn that they frequently accompany you also.

We always introduce them to our participants who find them very interesting. They learn many things from these young ladies. Being foreigners, the ladies illustrate the lessons about language and cultures very graphically. We will tell more about them later, but now allow us to share some of the lessons they illustrate.

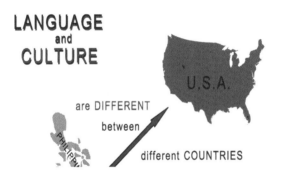

We must use an interpreter in Indonesia, and often in the Philippines. The need for interpreters exists in many different places we work. Without them we cannot communicate well. Different languages and cultures between nations have been a source of frustration for travelers throughout history. Awareness of the basic problems between nations may prevent disastrous and embarrassing results. Wars are often caused by simple conflicts in misunderstanding.

TRIBAL

The Philippines, where we conducted many of our seminars, is an archipelago country, consisting of thousands of islands. Each of these islands has its tribe or sub-tribe (some islands have many). Each tribe or group has its own language and culture. Depending upon the source, they say there are 87 to 126 distinctly different languages in the Philippines.

Between the tribes, and indeed between the dialects of the nation, many of the words are the same or similar. Many of their customs are also similar. There are two problems: totally different words, and same words with a totally different meaning. Which do you think would be most damaging: words or customs so different they cannot be understood, or words or customs that are similar or the same but have different meanings, causing confusion?

In the Philippine seminars we tell the story of the longest bridge in the world. We need to explain a little background for our non-Filipino readers. In Tagalog, the national language, *itlog* means egg, and *ebon* means bird. But in Pampanga *ebon* means egg. If you begin on the Pampanga end of the bridge carrying an *ebon* [egg], when you arrive on the other end of the bridge, your *ebon* is now a bird. Same word but different meanings. That makes it the longest bridge in the world. You begin walking on one side carrying an "egg" but when you arrive at the other end, you now have a "bird". Of course, the secret is the language. Two words; same pronunciation, but different meanings.

In one of the major languages of the Philippines a certain word means an ant that crawls on the ground, but in another major language used in another part of the archipelago, the same word means a bird that flies. You can imagine the disdain caused by asking the person to whom the word means "ant" if they would like to have one to eat although your meaning of the word is "bird".

In America, we have a sign for "OK" where we make a circle with the thumb and index finger. In the Philippines this same sign means "money." You can imagine the embarrassment caused were a man to use this sign toward a lady. It carries sexual overtones. In Germany it has a profane meaning. We were told that we had better not even mention this sign in Italy! The same cultural sign, but it has a widely different meaning. There are other signs and symbols used in different countries and cultures that cause the same confusion.

Three Young Ladies

Three young ladies earlier mentioned as our traveling companions love to be present in cross-cultural situations (which is why they are always with us). These ladies are:
> Mis-Understanding,
> Mis-Communication, and
> Mis-Trust.

It seems that they bring their own friends along with them, whom we will call "their boy friends":
> Disagreement,
> Division, and
> Hostility.

LANGUAGE
and
CULTURE
DIFFERENCES
INVITE THREE YOUNG LADIES

68

Like the woman of Proverbs 5:3-4, these may easily snare an unwary victim. *"For the lips of a strange woman drop as an honeycomb, and her mouth is smoother than oil: But her end is bitter as wormwood, sharp as a two edged sword"*. [KJV]

In fact, whenever two people have a conversation, the first two ladies will be present to some extent. When one talks, the idea in their mind is never exactly the same as the idea in the mind of the one listening. It is all right if the two young ladies remain quietly seated in the background. But when they start to take control of things, they invite the third young lady, mis-trust, to join them. Mis-trust brings their boyfriends, and they have a big party in your life. Their party makes a mess of things, and they do not clean up their own mess.

Whenever we have situations where the language and culture is different, these young ladies with their snares will also be found. They are always with us in our international travel!

In today's world, we must be aware of the need for sensitivity when dealing with people of another culture or language. It is too easy to become offensive without intending to be so when we are insensitive to what words may convey in cross-cultural situations. It is improper to beckon a person of Asian culture with the upraised finger. One is to be called to you with a downward motion of the whole hand. To beckon with the raised finger is to imply the person is a servant
.

CHRISTIAN AND NON-CHRISTIAN
Many of our seminars have participants who are interested in evangelism. One frequent expectation is to

learn to become more effective evangelists. We understand the basic truth that if someone speaks a language we don't know, we are unable to understand what is said. However, all too often we try to evangelize using uniquely Christian vocabulary. "Brother, are you born again?" Nicodemus was a religious leader of the day, and he did not understand what Jesus was talking about! Saved, salvation, and repentance are words that we usually learn the meaning of after we become Christians. We have heard some Christians witnessing using the word "propitiation". Many Christians don't even know what that one means.

If we are to present a relevant gospel, and not just invite others to join our group, we need to use language that is understandable. In the seminars we often have a time of group presentations of favorite ways to present the good news of Jesus Christ. The presentations are judged (by peers) on persuasiveness, relevance to a non-believer in the target community, and on understandable language. The participants are the primary teachers. If you are interested in evangelism, review your favorite methods of presenting the Gospel, and see if there are some uniquely Christian words, phrases, or ideas that a non-Christian might not understand.

DENOMINATIONAL
Another area relevant to the Christian where different languages and cultures exist is between denominations, between groups within a denomination, and even within a single church. If you find Disagreement, Division and Hostility, look for the three Mis-es, and we are sure you will find them. When you find them, you will find that majority of the mess can be cleaned up just by getting rid of the three young ladies!

70

They gather around our doctrines, rituals, and rules. These are the woof and warp of the fabric of our religious culture and language. As tribes living right next to one another may have major differences in language and culture, so will churches right next to one another, or committees in the same church. Just as people commonly migrate from one region to another (one tribe to another) in this mobile world, so in our Christian world, people move about freely between churches and denominations. They bring their own language and culture, and their own understandings. When these conflict with others, the three young ladies flourish!

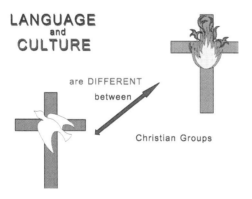

It is necessary for us to be aware of this language problem, and realize that many of our disagreements are caused by mis-understanding, mis-communication, producing mis-trust. When we are aware that this problem is always prevalent, we will seek the Holy Spirit's guidance to better interpretation of what is being said, and careful choice of words we use in communicating the gospel.

Terms and Definitions
Some of the words often used that present language problems in various cultures are listed with probable

definitions. You may think of other words or terms, and possibly other meanings.

Acid Test
A quick check that will verify if something is the real thing, and how good it is.

Born Again
1. The condition of a person who has received eternal life through Jesus Christ.
2. A sect of Christians in the Philippines, and maybe elsewhere. In Germany it refers to re-incarnational groups.

Charismatic
A person in a main-line traditional, denominational church, including Roman Catholic, whose religious practices include use of the gifts of the Spirit described in 1 Corinthians 12:8-10, and whose worship is at times physically demonstrative.

Doctrine
Man's understanding of God's Word. Comes from, but is not the same as, God's Word. For a Christian, God's Word is the Bible. For a non-Christian, the source of understanding is not the Bible.

Eternal Life
Having a personal relationship with God and Jesus Christ. See John 17:3.

Ministry
verb: 1. The act of touching others with God's love and power.
2. Use of the gifts of the Spirit found in Romans 12, 1 Corinthians 12, as well as other   places in the

Bible. Ministry may be to God or to people (individuals or groups). noun:
3. The vocation or avocation of following God's instructions.

Pentecostal

A person or group that believes and practices the "supernatural" gifts of the Spirit listed in 1 Corinthians 12:8-10, and whose worship is physically demonstrative. It may also refer to a person who belongs to the Pentecostal denomination.

Power Solution

A method or process of recognizing and eliminating a Power Stealer in our life.

Power Stealer

A practice that is contrary to the Word of God. It is particularly deceptive and hides completely from the one practicing it. It can be seen only by shining the light of the Word of God upon it.

Religion

The set of doctrines, rules, and rituals, by which a group worships their god.

Ritual

Something a group agrees to do together in a certain way. As soon as we agree on how we will worship God, we have a ritual. Every church therefore has rituals since they worship together by agreement. A ritual can be changed since it is only an agreement.

Rule
A guideline for behavior, which must be followed by a member of the group.

Saint
A believer in Jesus Christ. One who has been born again. One who has eternal life.

Spirit Filled
This one is too hot to touch. Read the chapters on Born Again and Spirit Filled.

Three Young Ladies
Mis-Understanding, Mis-Communication, and Mis-Trust. They are invited through cultural and language differences. They bring along their friends disagreement, division, and hostility.

Tradition
A ritual that has been practiced for some time. The length of time is not important, but the attitude toward the ritual is. A tradition is regarded as special by participants. By definition, a tradition may not be changed, since it would no longer be practiced the same way
You may wish to add to this list those words that have given you the greatest trouble and have caused problems in your communication and understanding.

THE BODY - EPHESIANS 4:11-12

"And He gave some, apostles; and some, prophets; and some, evangelists; and some, pastors and teachers; for the perfecting of the saints, for the work of the ministry, for the edifying of the body of Christ". [Eph 4: 11-12 KJV]

Perhaps the greatest error committed by the modern church is the sin of thievery. In our misunderstanding of what Jesus has given the Church, and His desire of the members of His Church, we have established a system whereby the Church is weakened, and the members are deprived of the Call of God being heard on their lives.

In our seminars Ephesians 4:11-12 is usually our opening scripture. As we study, the drawing emerges on the board or overhead as participants provide the answers from the lessons. We go phrase by phrase, or sometimes word by word through these two verses, analyzing what we think against what St Paul actually says. To get the most from this lesson, answer the questions before you read the answers.

Before we start the study, please think about your church and its organization. Then answer these questions.

Whose job is it in your church (a specific name, please) to:
        pray for the sick;
        visit the prisons;
        counsel those with problems;
        provide for members with needs;
        follow-up visit to newcomers

These are all examples of ministry.

Now to our study:

EPHESIANS 4:11-12 *"And He gave some, apostles; and some, prophets; and some, evangelists; and some, pastors and teachers; for the perfecting of the saints, for the work of the ministry, for the edifying of the body of Christ"* [KJV]

One of my favorite methods of pulling meaning from the Bible is finding action words. I believe the Bible is alive and active, and calls us to action. Action words are keys that can unlock meaning.

What is the first action word in verse 11?
Who is it doing it?
You must look at the text before verse 11 to learn that it is talking about Jesus.
Our study starts with our Lord and Savior, Jesus Christ. *"It was he"* refers to Jesus.
Jesus gave!

What did Jesus give?
Jesus gave apostles, prophets, evangelists, pastors, and teachers. Upon consideration you will find that these are people.

In relationship to the church, what do we call these people?

These are church **leaders.** These five leadership positions are often called the **5-fold ministry** of the church. Participants often answer "Ministers," "Servants of God," or "church workers." What do you commonly call them? If you are teaching, get the participants to answer this question if you can. The lesson is more powerful that way. Some groups will not have any understanding and will not come up with the answers, so you will have to just tell them.

Ephesians 4:12
"to prepare God's people for works of service, so that the body of Christ may be built up"- NIV.

What is the leaders' job according to this scripture? (verb or action word)?
Prepare, or equip

Who do the leaders prepare?
God's People.

What are God's people supposed to do?
Works of service (or ministry, depending upon the translation.

What is the result of the ministry?
The body of Christ is built up. Notice this happens with internal, personal growth as a result of the ministry to one another, and also in terms of size, or numbers as those outside the body are brought in.

Observations and Comments
Now look at the completed drawing of this scripture and ask for comments or observations. One of the first that will emerge will be that the body has no head. This is because the head is not mentioned in this scripture. We find the head in verse 15.

EPH 4:15 *"Instead, speaking the truth in love, we will in all things grow up into him who is the Head, that is, Christ".* – NIV

Who is the head?

Christ, the head of the body. We have now come full circle.

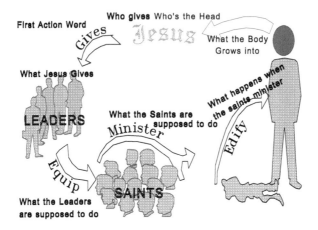

Does the head need to grow?

No, He is already perfect!

Review: Christ **gives** leaders to the Church (or Body of Christ).

The leaders **prepare** God's people.

God's people **serve, or minister**

The Body of Christ **builds** itself up to the fullness of Christ, the head.

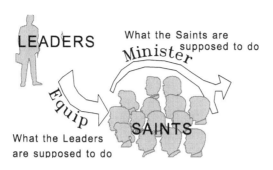

LEADERS

What the Saints are supposed to do

Minister

Equip

What the Leaders are supposed to do

SAINTS

To be a Christian is to be a minister. All Christians are supposed to be in ministry. Many Christians do not understand this, and many churches do not teach this. There are many aspects to this. The first is introduced here: we think that it is the church leaders' job to minister, not the "ordinary" Christian's. For the Church to function as Scripture expresses Jesus' desire is, we must change our understanding.

The Bible here and elsewhere clearly states that the Body of Christ (the church) grows when every member ministers. Yet by experience in more than 50 seminars (usually 5-8 churches), only three churches have answered the question, "In your church, whose job is it to . . ." with the name of a lay person. The others answered that it was the job of their paid (or sometimes unpaid) staff (usually only the pastor in the small rural churches). No wonder our churches fail to grow!

Look at your answer to the questions about "Whose job is it to... "? we started with. Are the names those of paid ministry staff, or of church members? [Note to teachers: If the class has answered the questions with names of lay people, they will be unusual, and will not demonstrate the lesson].

While the Bible is clear about the **ministry of the laity,** we even call these five leadership positions **"The Five-Fold Ministry."** This scripture passage says the saints are the ministry, the leaders (or offices) mentioned are for equipping, or perfecting, not ministry. In our very speech, we exhibit that we do not read what it really says, but what we have been taught. You may object, saying, "They are only semantics." Practice in the churches reveals the accuracy of speech and the power of words.

The content, or information, of our misunderstanding the Bible in this passage demonstrates another problem. In the churches paid staff is ministering while most of the people sit and watch and listen. Seminar participants agree that our leaders seem to no longer be leaders given by Christ but employees hired by the people **to do** the ministry. When the "employee" pastor does not do what the congregation "employer" desires, they fire the pastor and hire a new one! Thank God the Charismatic Episcopal Church does not permit the church members to "employ" their priest. He is appointed by the Bishop as the one **called** to serve the flock.

Spectator Sports

Consider basketball (or you can use football, whatever is more well known in your location). In a normal popular game, there are ten people playing at one time, with a couple of referees (maybe coaches too) active. There are thousands watching, cheering, booing or just watching. In seminars the very highest estimate of active members was 75% (not including one pastor who said 100% - he had no members). The average is somewhere around 15% of church members who are in ministry.

We will take the very highest, and make that our example. One fourth of the team is paralyzed, unable to move. They are not just injured or tired, but paralyzed. Do you think that our team could reach the championships? Probably not. We Christians are on the winning team. I know, I read the end of the book. How can we ever hope to be a winning team with 25% paralyzed? Or worse, how can we hope to win with 85% paralyzed?

I admit there are many more people active in the game than just the ones we see playing. There are the trainers, the ball boys, the statisticians, the substitutes (bench warmers), and many others who make the game of basketball. But the great majority watch. Basketball is a spectator sport.

I also admit that in the church there are many working that are not easily seen. There are the quiet prayer warriors, the unsung janitors, altar guild, and sound and setup people. Still, the great majority is watching, just as in basketball. Christianity, however, is not a spectator sport. The Bible says believers are to be ministering, not observing. Many churches today are not victorious just because of this Power Stealer principle.

There are three types of Church workers:
1. Hireling - paid to work
2. Volunteer - works so long as no conflict with personal interests
3. Servant - a volunteer who is committed first to task given by the Lord

Full-Time Minister?

In the 1994 Indonesian National Convention of the Full Gospel Business Men International, I presented a modified version of this module. Many in the group of nearly a thousand admitted that they felt guilty. They felt somehow that they needed to quit their jobs to really be in ministry.

This has destroyed many who, knowing they are called into ministry, quit their jobs because that is the only thing they knew as "ministry". Where did they learn this? Not from the Bible! Others are paralyzed because they know they should be in ministry, but the church teaches that they are not in ministry unless they are "full-time" ministers - ordained! They are not allowed to minister boldly, because they are not professional or vocational ministers.

For ten years before I [Hugh Kaiser] became a full-time **missionary** I was a full-time minister. When my seven-year Indonesian management project was finished, I produced a picture project book. They use these books like we Americans use our school year books, asking for comments and signatures. The managers requested me to write spiritual blessings in their project books. Even the Muslims knew I was a minister of God's blessings.

A few months later, when I left my job, the boss said that he would miss me. When I was not in the office, if some of the staff did not feel well, they would go home and be gone the rest of the day, maybe longer. When I was in the office, they got up, came back to my desk, and in three minutes were back at work. Prayer was their answer. I knew, and they knew, that I was in full-time ministry.

In the seminars, we point out that in verses 13, 14, and 15 the author Paul, himself an equipper, an Apostle, places himself among the believers as a minister with them, and as needing to be perfected with them. As a saint, or believer, Paul ministers. As an Apostle, he equips the believers to minister.

Two Great Problems

There are two major concerns in allowing people to minister. The first is that they may make mistakes since they lack the training we would like them to have. The leader can do the job much better than the Alay person. (Incidentally, I don't think you can find the distinction between clergy and laity in the Bible in so far as who is to minister.)

Able or Available?

In those early days in the Philippines, I came to realize that it was my availability, not my ability, through which God works. Many times they would refuse to have an interpreter, insisting they spoke English. I knew well that they really couldn't understand, from their answers to simple questions in general conversation.

One time, after teaching in the hot afternoon, with participants who were often dozing off and whose English ability was suspect, I asked if there were questions. They began to ask questions relevant to their worship services, relevant to their relatives and friends, to life in general. The teaching was on the power of the Holy Spirit and was new to them. It was the same teaching I had brought to sophisticated professionals in America, who though they understood every word, did not comprehend what I was saying.

These rural Filipinos, who could not have understood most of my words, understood clearly that the Lord had something more for them, and they were eager not only to learn about it, but also to receive it. Often I am convinced that it does not matter what I say, the Holy Spirit will speak to them and teach them!

We do not need to fear that the results will be less because the ability is less. In fact God accomplishes the work in and through each of us (1Cor 12:6) through our availability, not our ability. The Apostle Paul claimed that when He was weak, then God could make him strong! *"Therefore I take pleasure in infirmities, in reproaches, in necessities, in persecutions, in distresses for Christ's sake: for when I am weak, then am I strong."* [2 Cor 12:10 KJV] And God is always the same! The important thing is that we serve Him with all our heart.

Second Great Danger
The second great danger in allowing us "ordinary" Christians to minister is that we might be better than the leader! If this were to be discovered, then who would need the leader? This could be a great problem for a leader! Many leaders do keep the people in bondage, fearing that the people will discover they do not really need him!

I belong to a small local church, focused on simple ministry locally. It would be very possible for my priest to feel threatened when I come home, since some think this itinerant international ministry is quite glamorous. My priest is very supportive and gives me every opportunity to minister at home. He knows his calling and he is eager to see me, as well as the others under his care, equipped for the ministry, to the glory of God.

84

Fear Gets Us All!

The leaders are not the only ones paralyzed by **Fear.** Every Christian is affected. Fear of making a mistake, of appearing foolish in the eyes of peers or leaders often prevents us from acting. Surely, we need to have training and instruction, but surely God will work with power if we will but make ourselves available. He will provide the ability. It is His promise!

ENABLING MINISTRIES

A way in which we may further understand the role of those we often assign the title "minister" is in re-interpreting their role as the **enablers** who call out and prepare those who will be the ministers.

First, St Paul says, Christ gives the **Apostle** to the Church. Think of him as the Skeleton of the body, the Structure of the Church. In the early church the Apostle of course was the one who began the new congregation, and in many places today in the Charismatic Episcopal Church it is again the bishop who is doing the church planting. The bishop, as the successor of the first apostles, provides the visible structure for the church, hence the statement "where the bishop is there is the Church."

Second, the **Prophet** is the voice of encouragement providing feeling and vitality to the Church. He is like the Nervous System of the physical body. He provides the incentive for action. On one occasion I [Philip Weeks] was worshiping in a church, and upon leaving, passed the room where a young lady was singing. She was rehearsing a song, and her voice captivated my attention. I stood outside the room without her knowing I was present, and listened to her lovely voice. I was back at that church at a later date, and it was the Sunday she was appointed to sing this particular song during the offertory. Her offering that morning did not compare favorably with what I had heard on the earlier rehearsal. She was nervous, and it was obvious in her mannerism and her voice. When she finished the song, she returned to her seat and her countenance revealed her estimation of her singing. She was not pleased with herself. As soon as the Eucharist ended, I quickly went to her. I thanked her for her offering. I told her I had heard her rehearsal several Sundays before and how thankful to God I was for His allowing me to be present to hear her sing. I told her how blessed I was by hearing her. I complimented her lovely voice, and encouraged her to continue blessing people. In saying those things, I exhorted her to give her best, and I strengthened her for another time.. In 1 Corinthians 14: 3, St Paul lists three benefits of prophecy: to edify, to exhort, to strengthen! One of our Filipina students related the story of her first and only time to sing in church. After arriving back home that evening, her mother told her how poorly she did. She never sang again!

The **Evangelist** is the third enabler and he may be compared to the Digestive System in the physical body. His ministry is to send throughout the Body the blessings of the Evangel, the Good News, so those who hear the good news of Jesus Christ may be equipped to share the message with others. That which is consumed nourishes the Body of Christ and feeds others as well.

Fourth is the **Pastor** and he is comparable to the Circulatory System. As the physical body is fed through the blood stream, the pastor finds good solid food to feed the members so they may be properly prepared to enter the mission field of the world.

Finally comes the **Teacher** who trains the Mind in the things of God. One of the marks of the early church in Acts 2: 42 was the continuation in the Apostles' teaching. For us today this is Bible study. Many Christians are without victory because they never open the Bible to study the Promises of God. When Satan comes to rob them of God's blessings, they lack the knowledge by which to combat him. When Satan tempted Jesus after His time of fasting, His weapon was, "it is written", and he quoted the Scriptures He had in His time.

A vital part of the Body is missing in this analogy. It is the Respiratory System, represented by the Holy Spirit. Many churches appear lifeless because the Holy Spirit is unrecognized. The Spirit gives life, and as the respiratory system provides the necessary breath for physical life, so the Spirit provides the breath necessary for a church to be alive.

These ministry gifts are given for the purpose of enabling the members of the Church to discover and functionally use their gifts for the building up of the Body.

WHAT IT MEANS TO BE BORN AGAIN?

We have introduced the three young ladies and how they bring confusion and division into our lives because of differences in language and culture. This is true not only between nations and tribes, but is also true between different groups of Christians. For this reason we look at the scriptural meaning of some Christian terms which different groups understand quite differently.

The term "born again" is a popular Christian phrase. Unfortunately, there is much misunderstanding about its meaning. It is one of those phrases that mean different things in different Christian cultures. In the seminars I point out how the different "denominational languages" create barriers between Christian groups and individuals. I often have the participants write out a short definition of the term "born again" to demonstrate the point.

Write your own one-sentence definition of born again on a sheet of paper so you can compare. It may enlighten you to do this exercise.

Examples of answers I have heard include:
"Someone who believes in Jesus."
"Someone who has repented from sin, accepted Jesus in his heart, and has been baptized."
"Someone who has received the Holy Spirit."
"Someone who has received the Holy Spirit as evidenced by speaking in tongues."
"Someone who has been saved and speaks in tongues."

"Someone who has received Christ and lives a holy life."

Sometimes, the answer reveals the denominational training a person has had. The definitions shown above demonstrate some theological confusion. In the Philippines "Born Again" is a sect. In Germany it refers to those who believe in re-incarnation. In Africa it usually means one who no longer smokes or drinks. The confusion is revealed by the comparison of definitions and hopefully dispelled when we begin to examine the biblical description of the term. The exercise and subsequent Bible study confirms that we don't understand all we read.

ORIGIN

The term was used by Jesus to explain spiritual things to Nicodemus, a Jewish leader.

"There was a man of the Pharisees, named Nicodemus, a ruler of the Jews: The same came to Jesus by night, and said unto him, Rabbi, we know that thou art a teacher come from God: for no man can do these miracles that thou doest, except God be with him. Jesus answered and said unto him, Verily, verily, I say unto thee, except a man be born again, he cannot see the kingdom of God. Nicodemus saith unto him, how can a man be born when he is old? can he enter the second time into his mother's womb, and be born? Jesus answered, Verily, verily, I say unto thee, except a man be born of water and of the Spirit, he cannot enter into the kingdom of God. That which is born of the flesh is flesh; and that which is born of the Spirit is spirit."
[JOHN 3:1-6 KJV]

Jesus made it clear that even though we have been born of the flesh (through our mother), we must be born of the Spirit for us to enter the Kingdom of God. The capital

S indicates that this refers to the Holy Spirit, the lower case s is for other spirits, in this case the human spirit. The Bible shows us why this Spiritual birth is necessary as well as what it is. For our study, we begin with the beginning, in Genesis.

MAN IN GOD'S IMAGE

GENESIS 1:26 "And God said, "Let us make man in our image, after our likeness." - [NIV].
        God is a triune being: Father, Son, and Holy Spirit. We see three parts named. One is a central being, essence, one is in bodily form, another one is Spirit. Man also has three parts: a central thinking unit (mind or soul), plus a body, and a spirit.

1 Thessalonians 5:23 *"May God himself, the God of peace, sanctify you through and through. May your whole spirit, soul and body be kept blameless at the coming of our Lord Jesus Christ."* NIV

JOB 32:8 *"But it is the spirit in a man, the breath of the Almighty,that gives him understanding."* NIV

It is with the spirit in man that God's Spirit has communication and communion, just as it is with the body that communication with the world takes place. Our mind or soul is between, and contains our emotions, our reasoning, and our will. God can speak to our mind (as can Satan) but true communion does not take place there. Our spirit provides the doorway to communion with God.

JOHN 4:24 *"God is spirit, and his worshipers must worship in spirit and in truth."* NIV If God is spirit, and man was originally made in the image of God, it means that

90

man was a spirit, that happened to have a body and mind (or soul).

DEATH THAT REQUIRES RE-BIRTH

There was only one rule that Adam and Eve had to follow in the Garden of Eden: "Don't Eat!" (Gen. 2:17). It appears that they did not die right away (Gen 5:4). But just as looks were deceiving when Eve saw that the forbidden fruit was good to eat, it is also deceiving to assume that just because a person is walking and talking that this person is really alive, in the Biblical and true sense.

JAMES 2:26 *"As the body without the spirit is dead, so faith without deeds is dead.* "NIV

JOHN 6:53 *"Jesus said to them, "I tell you the truth, unless you eat the flesh of the Son of Man and drink his blood, you have no life in you."* NIV

They became dead to God!

Even though it seems obvious that a person is alive, that person may not be. If we look at the model, we can see what happens. With the original sin, the door between man and God was shut. Our spirit was deprived of the life-giving Holy Spirit.

Adam and Eve did die! The spirit being died. They were no longer spirit beings, but flesh beings who had no ability to commune with God in the spirit.

THE RE-BIRTH

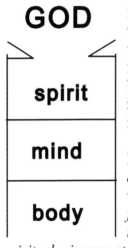

GOD

spirit

mind

body

The Christian has been raised from the dead along with Christ. Now the door is opened again and fellowship with God is possible. The Holy Spirit fills us and gives our spirit life, and we become spirit beings, new creations, as man was originally created and intended to be all along.

Ephesians 2:1 *"As for you, you were dead in your transgressions and sins, in which you used to live when you followed the ways of this world and of the ruler of the kingdom of the air, the spirit who is now at work in those who are disobedient."* NIV

Here the writer Paul refers to living, breathing people as being dead in sin, and gives the reason and circumstance: they were following the ways of Satan.

Being born again means that the Spirit of God has breathed life into your dead spirit through accepting Jesus Christ's death as payment to purchase you from the former owner, Satan. The purpose of being Born Again of the Spirit of God is to replace the dominion where it belongs, under God with man as the manager in charge. This repositioning of submission and authority allows man to again have a personal relationship with God, as before "the fall." Without it, man cannot have this relationship; cannot "enter the kingdom of God."

This is why Jesus said, "You must be born again."

Ephesians 2:4-5 *"But because of his great love for us, God, who is rich in mercy, made us alive with Christ even when we were dead in transgressions--it is by grace you have been saved."* NIV

Col 2:13 *"When you were dead in your sins and in the un-circumcision of your sinful nature, God made you alive with Christ. He forgave us all our sins."* NIV

This is what Jesus called being "born again." Jesus declared, *"I tell you the truth, no one can see the kingdom of God unless he is born again."*

"You should not be surprised at my saying, 'You must be born again". NIV

BORN AGAIN AND THE HOLY SPIRIT

I have had seminar participants who were confused about the relationship of the Holy Spirit and being Born Again. In this lesson we do not teach about the Holy Spirit, except to point out that one who has been "born again" is also "saved," or has "eternal life," and "has the Holy Spirit" (all these are Christian language words or phrases which have varying meanings).   Jesus connected the Holy Spirit and eternal life in John 4:13-14: *Jesus answered, "Everyone who drinks this water will be thirsty again, but whoever drinks the water I give him will never thirst. Indeed, the water I give him will become in him a spring of water welling up to eternal life."* NIV

Compare this measure of the Holy Spirit (filled to eternal life) with another measure mentioned in John 7:38-39 *"Whoever believes in me, as the Scripture has said, streams of living water will flow from within him." By this he meant the Spirit, whom those who believed in him were later to receive. Up to that time the Spirit had not been given, since Jesus had not yet been glorified."*   NIV

WHAT DOES IT MEAN?

We have seen in John 4:14 that people who believe on Jesus are filled with living water to eternal life. In John 17: 3 it is recorded that in His prayer the night before He was betrayed, Jesus gave a definition of eternal life. *"Now this is eternal life: that they may know you, the only true God, and Jesus Christ, whom you have sent."* NIV

Most languages have two words for the English word "know." One means to know information, the other means to know a person, have a relationship. The word that is used here is the relationship "know". This lesson becomes very powerful when I ask Filipinos or Indonesians (whose languages have different "know" words) what their local words are. Then they examine the scripture carefully, and the reality of what it says sinks in. In Christ we meet God. We know Him. We have a relationship with Him.

I often use the illustration of the President. I ask how many know about him. Everyone raises the hand. They know about him from television, papers, and other media. They have seen pictures of him, heard stories about him. They know that every national decision he makes affects their lives. He is their President.

When I ask how many know the President, sometimes some hands go up. I ask how they know the President. They say they have met him sometime, shook hands with him. We are very aware if we know the President or not, whether we have ever met him or not. The same is true of Christianity. If Christianity is a relationship with God, then we should know that we have indeed met him, know Him. We can know many things about Him from the Bible, from sermons, from pictures and stories we have heard. This does not mean that we know him. We know him if we have met him.

Sometimes in seminars there are participants who realize that they have never met Him. They really do not have a relationship with Him. We have had pastors and leaders in high church positions come to this realization. All their lives they have learned about Jesus, but no one told them they should meet Him, and they never had. They knew a lot, but they did not know the God. We always give opportunity to reflect on when and how the participants met God, and if they have not, give them an opportunity to meet Him. We give them an opportunity to be Born Again.

HOW TO BE BORN AGAIN

In the next chapter we explore the second measure, the filling to overflowing rivers of living water. Right now, let's consider carefully how one can become born again. In the seminar, I let the participants list all the requirements. As we agreed in the beginning, these requirements must be confirmed with scripture. Since the seminars are mostly with pastors and church leaders, usually they are familiar with at least their favorite scriptures on the topic.

As the sample definitions at the beginning of this chapter indicate, there are also some different opinions about the requirements. The usual scriptures that come from groups include:

Acts 2:38, Acts 2:38 *"Peter replied, "Repent and be baptized, every one of you, in the name of Jesus Christ for the forgiveness of your sins. And you will receive the gift of the Holy Spirit.* " NIV (repent, and be baptized. Result will receive the Spirit)

Acts 2:41 *"Those who accepted his message were baptized, and about three thousand were added to their number that day."* NIV

Acts 16:30- 31 *"He then brought them out and asked, "Sirs, what must I do to be saved?" They replied, "Believe in the Lord Jesus, and you will be saved--you and your household."* - NIV

Romans 10:9-10 *"That if you confess with your mouth, "Jesus is Lord," and believe in your heart that God raised him from the dead, you will be saved. For it is with your heart that you believe and are justified, and it is with your mouth that you confess and are saved."* NIV

Mark 16:16 *"Whoever believes and is baptized will be saved, but whoever does not believe will be condemned."* NIV.

Romans 6:3 *"Or don't you know that all of us who were baptized into Christ Jesus were baptized into his death?"* NIV

Gal 3:26-27 *"You are all sons of God through faith in Christ Jesus, for all of you who were baptized into Christ have clothed yourselves with Christ."* NIV

The requirements above include:
  believing in Jesus,
  confessing Jesus as Lord,
  receiving Jesus,
  having faith in Jesus,

and baptism.
We have yet to find any reference scripture for additional requirements! There are no other requirements to enter the door to eternal life. This is important to remember as we continue our discussion, especially when we talk about maturity and ministry. Like our ancestors all the way to Adam and Eve, we cannot see or enter the Kingdom of God without it. With it, we obtain the free pass.

In the seminars, we usually refer to Romans 10: 9-10 which says if you believe in your heart and confess with your mouth that Jesus is Lord, you will be saved. We invite participants to reconfirm (or declare for the first time) that Jesus is Lord, and invite Him to live in our hearts, to be more real every day.

It may be that you are reading this, and you realize that even though you know about Jesus, you have never invited Him to be your Lord and Savior. You have never experienced a relationship with Him. If this is true, and you would like to experience a relationship with Him, you can pray this simple prayer:

"God, I know that I can never come to you by the good works that I do. I could never earn the right to be in Your presence. I am condemned to spiritual death by sin. I believe that you came to earth as a man in Jesus, and died that I might live with you. I believe that you were resurrected and that by the same resurrection power I can be resurrected to life with You. I accept the free gift of this salvation by Jesus' blood, and I receive Jesus to be my Lord and Savior. Jesus, I invite you into my life, to change my life, to truly be my Lord as well as Savior. Amen."

Some other scriptures often used by participants in reference to "born again" demonstrate Bible Blindness and the principle of not knowing as much as we think we know. John 1:12 and Revelation 3:20 are frequently used by evangelists to invite people to be born again. A careful reading of both those scriptures will reveal that neither one refers to unbelievers being born again at all. John 1:12 is addressed to the Jewish contemporaries of Jesus who met Him and received Him and they received the right to become sons of God. Revelation 3:20 does not refer to Jesus standing at the door of unbelievers. Jesus is the door for unbelievers. This verse refers to Christians who have locked Jesus out of His Church.

A powerful teaching tool for training people in evangelism is what some call "the Bridge Model.

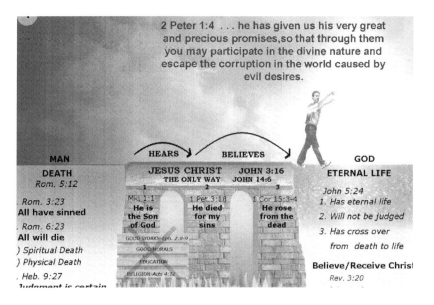

Jesus becomes the BRIDGE between eternal death and eternal life. In accepting Him as Savior we pass from death into life. He is the only way - John 14:6. If in teaching this model of evangelism it is best to draw on the board two columns with a chasm between. One column is Eternal Death; the other is Eternal Life. The chasm represents the Lake of Fire or the Second death spoken of in Revelation 21:8. Jesus bridges the chasm by His death and resurrection. Man is created for God's pleasure and promised Eternal Life, but in his sin of disobedience he gets Eternal Death. Jesus is the BRIDGE that saves us from the Second and final death - separation from God.

We will not elaborate on **The Four Spiritual Laws** since it has been widely used, other than to mention it briefly. It provides a wonderful outline in which a person can give their personal testimony as a witnessing tool:

1. God loves you and has a plan for your life.
2. Man is a sinner!
3. Jesus Christ is God's answer to man's sin problem.
4. Acceptance of Jesus as Savior is necessary for eternal life.

There are other models that can be effectively used to illustrate to the seeker the Love of God and His salvation plan through Jesus Christ. Some simple models are occasionally demonstrated in our seminars that cannot be illustrated here. One is the **Ticket-to-Heaven** model, where a piece of paper is specially folded. The illustrator tells a story that includes a Christian seeking to tell the salvation story to an unbeliever. The unbeliever hasn't time to listen and the Christian leaves. En route to his home the Christian is struck and killed in an accident and finds himself walking on a road. Suddenly he meets the unbeliever coming toward him. He too has died since the Christian was at his house. The unbeliever sees the Christian holding in his hand a piece of paper that they conclude to be the believer's Ticket to Heaven. The unbeliever decides to walk along with the believer and asks that he share a piece of his ticket. A portion is torn and given to the unbeliever who isn't satisfied with the little he has and asks for more. At the entrance to Heaven, St Peter requires the producing of each person's ticket. The unbeliever produces his bits of torn paper and when they are unfolded and laid out they spell **HELL**. The believer's paper is unfolded and it is a **Cross**. The message is that one cannot get to heaven on someone else's ticket. You must have your own.

Another model that can't be illustrated here but frequently used in the seminars is what we call the **Dirty Water** model. We take a glass partially filled with dirty water, and by pouring clean water in to overflow, we force out the dirty water, thus illustrating how the Holy Spirit's entering the seeker's life brings in His cleansing and purification.

Methodology of Church Evangelism:

Some effective ways of evangelism include:
1. House/cell group ministry
    The church membership is divided into cell or house groups for purposes of study, prayer, personal ministry in the Holy Spirit, and use this as a tool for equipping the members in sharing their faith. The house meeting may also be a place to which unbelievers are invited when they may not go to the church building. They may be formed according to geographical location.

2. Radio/Television ministry
    This is expensive but apparently effective, but often the results not known.

3. Neighborhood Prayer and visitation

Some Charismatic Episcopal Churches have committed themselves to "taking their city" for Christ, and will target areas in their service domicile where members walk, praying for each house or store. They may follow up by distributing information about their church. When standing in front of a house and praying, should someone come up and question them, it is the opportune time to share the good news.

4. Healing services

People appreciate prayer in times of illness, and it provides an opportunity to tell the story of Jesus' love.

5. Tract distribution

Make certain the tract presents the gospel in a non-offensive manner.

6. Testimony

Perhaps in an appropriate place in the liturgy such as following the Epistle, a person can give testimony of answered prayer, making the testimony a present-day epistle.

7. Exciting people

The best way to evangelize is through getting people excited about their Faith and their Church. They will tell others. We often emphasize that Shepherds [pastors] do not reproduce sheep, but sheep reproduce sheep. Pastors who train their church members on how to share their faith will find them bringing new people to a personal relationship with Jesus.

PREPARING A TESTIMONY!

Many people have a wonderful testimony of what the Lord has done in their life, but don't know how to share it. A testimony is the sign of God's life at work in our midst. If there is no testimony, it is a sign of God's abiding life being absent in a congregation. We always need to be prepared to give others the reason for what they may find different about us.

There are some things to remember. First, a testimony is about Jesus, not yourself. Second, a testimony is not preaching but simply sharing. It has power to bring people to Jesus Christ. It is non-debatable since it is your personal experience. The listener may accept it or reject it, but it is your personal experience.

When I [Philip Weeks] am doing evangelism workshops in churches, one of the things I like to include is a morning exercise when participants write their testimony. I carefully walk the seminar participants through eleven steps, some of which may be redundant, but nevertheless listed so that everything necessary will be included.

I specify how much should be said about each category so that the most important will be emphasized and the least important minimized. The testimony can be about any event in one's life where they have experienced the Presence of God in a life changing way. It may be a healing testimony, an answer to prayer, or their salvation experience.

Step 1. What were the circumstances of your life at the time you had this experience? Write two sentences describing this.

102

Step 2. What was your attitude at the time you had this experience? Were you searching for a relationship with God, or seeking answers to some questions? Again, two sentences.

Step 3. What was the setting? Were you at home, in the hospital, in church, alone or with someone? One sentence will suffice.

Step 4. Was there someone who was helpful in your having this experience? Again, one sentence.

Step 5. How was Jesus revealed to you? Explain in detail and you may use as many as ten sentences to describe this revelation.

Step 6. Did someone say something that made a difference, resulting in this experience? Two sentences are used to describe this.

Step 7. Was there a special scripture? Limit yourself to three verses. To go beyond this might turn off the listener, and they get the impression that you are a Bible quote. Your task is to share Jesus, not impress others upon your memorization of Scripture.

Step 8. What kind of response did you make? What was the result of your initial response? Did you feel emotion? What kind of thoughts did you have? What caused you to make your response? This is the climatic part of the testimony and as many as twenty sentences may be used.

Step 9. Did you pray? What did you pray? How did you pray? No more than five sentences.

Step 10. How did your encounter with God change you? Were you immediately aware of Him in your life? Use up to five sentences to describe this.

Step 11. What difference is it making now? Again, five-sentence limit.

It is good to write out your testimony, practice it in the solitude of your home, and then share it with a person you trust who will react constructively to what you have written. A testimony is like a road map; it shows you where you are going and how to get there. Sometimes you may take short cuts and other times you may travel the more elaborate scenic route.

Closure:

As I ask you now, you may conclude your testimony by asking the hearer if they have had a personal relationship with Jesus? This is my question to you, dear reader. Do you know about Him or know Him? Knowledge about Him is insufficient. He wants us to know Him as He knows us. If you do not know Him, now is the perfect moment to say, "Come into my life and take control, Lord Jesus. Forgive me all my sins, and fill me with your life giving Spirit."

WHAT IT MEANS TO BE SPIRIT FILLED

This is another phrase in the Christian vocabulary around which the three young ladies congregate with their escorts. There is much confusion and disagreement preventing unity in the Body of Christ today over this term. We do not teach all about the Holy Spirit but we establish a common vocabulary and understanding of the purpose(s) of the filling of the Holy Spirit. We see how misunderstanding between groups causes divisions and hostility or fear.

As with Born Again, it is helpful to write out your own definition of "Spirit Filled." When teaching this information it is important to compare the class' definitions.

John 7:38,39
Rivers of Living Water Flow

From the key scripture, John 7:38, we see that this living water which will fill one to everlasting life (John 4:13-14) can also flow out of a believer. From verse 39, we see the explanation of the living water as the Holy Spirit who will be given from above after Jesus is glorified.

John 7:38-39 "*He that believeth on me, as the scripture hath said, out of his belly shall flow rivers of living water. (But this spake he of the Spirit, which they that believe on him should receive:*

105

for the Holy Ghost was not yet given; because that Jesus was not yet glorified.)" KJV

John 16:7 *"Nevertheless I tell you the truth; It is expedient for you that I go away: for if I go not away, the Comforter will not come unto you; but if I depart, I will send him unto you."* KJV

What is the difference between these two measures of the Holy Spirit?

John 4 clearly states the purpose: eternal life. The purpose of the second measure, the out- flowing, is clear from other scriptures, but we can see it in this example. If I have rivers of living water flowing out of me, what will happen to the person who comes near me? They will get wet, of course. They will be wet with the Spirit of God, maybe even filled to eternal life. We can see then, that the purpose of this out flowing is so we can be salt and light in the world, so we can be a witness to Jesus.

This is expressed in Acts 1:8 *"But you will receive power when the Holy Spirit comes on you; and you will be my witnesses in Jerusalem, and in all Judea and Samaria, and to the ends of the earth."* NIV

APPLICATION TO UNITY

Consider now the person who experiences this out flowing for the first time. The presence of the living God is so real! The miracles, which happen with the out flowing as the healing power of the Holy Spirit touches others, is exciting! Someone has said that persons experiencing the Holy Spirit for their first time should be shut in a closet for six months. Many go around grabbing friends by their

106

jacket lapels and shouting in their face: "You need the Holy Spirit!" "Conservative" denominations do not understand and are fearful of this movement because they have seen excesses. They have seen harmful effects, while failing to see fruit produced in the lives of these "charismatics."

If you are a Charismatic or Pentecostal, consider this information when you wish to share your joy with your conservative friends. If you are a conservative, consider this information when your friends accost you. First, anyone born again has been filled with the Holy Spirit, by definition of John 4:14, to eternal life. If they are told, "you need the Holy Spirit," they will cease to listen further, because they know the person talking does not know what they are talking about (different language, you see). He knows he is already filled with the Spirit (to eternal life).

If you wish to share an experience of the Lord, please remember that the other person may have a different language and culture. The other will be able to hear you if you speak his language. If not, how can he possibly understand? Even worse, if your words have different meaning to him, he will mis-understand. Here come the three young ladies, just waiting for that invitation to bring their friends disagreement, division, and hostility. And remember, John, Peter, Andrew, and each of the disciples had different relationships with Jesus. Neither should we expect everyone to have the same relationship, the same experiences with Him.

TWO MEASURES: VALID DOCTRINE?

We see in the Born Again chapter how God breathes life into the human spirit, causing him to be a new creation (2 Corinithians 5:17), that is a spirit being rather

107

than a flesh being, enabling communion with Him. Thus we understand that one who has new life in Christ is filled with the Holy Spirit (living water), to eternal life. We see now a second measure - that of living water flowing out. Are these really two separate measures? Is this really a valid doctrine (our understanding of the Word of God)? Let's look to the basic manual, the Word of God.

Acts 8:14-19 *"When the apostles in Jerusalem heard that Samaria had accepted the word of God, they sent Peter and John to them. When they arrived, they prayed for them that they might receive the Holy Spirit, because the Holy Spirit had not yet come upon any of them; they had simply been baptized into the name of the Lord Jesus. Then Peter and John placed their hands on them, and they received the Holy Spirit.*

When Simon saw that the Spirit was given at the laying on of the apostles' hands, he offered them money and said, Give me also this ability so that everyone on whom I lay my hands may receive the Holy Spirit." NIV

Here we see that the people became believers and were baptized. Few would argue that at this point they were not yet Christians, that they had not yet received the gift of eternal life. They do have the Holy Spirit otherwise they could not have gotten the eternal life. Yet, something is missing, and the apostles came from Jerusalem, laid their hands on them and prayed, and they received that "something", or that "something" was released in their lives. Later, we will look at that "something" and what the results should be if we have it, or if it is released in us. To me the argument of "have" or "have not" is irrelevant. The question is, is it working in and through us? It can and should be.

108

The first measure we cannot see from the outside. People say they believe and they submit to baptism. We cannot see living water within. The second measure is evident through some undisclosed immediate evidence that even the magician Simon can see. Onlookers can see waters flowing out.

In Acts 9, Ananias is sent to lay hands on Saul (later called Paul) in order that he might receive the Holy Spirit. After this, Saul is baptized.

Acts 9:17-18 *"Then Ananias went to the house and entered it. Placing his hands on Saul, he said, "Brother Saul, the Lord--Jesus, who appeared to you on the road as you were coming here--has sent me so that you may see again and be filled with the Holy Spirit.."*
Acts 9:18 *"Immediately something like scales fell from Saul's eyes, and he could see again. He got up and was baptized."* NIV

In Acts 10, Cornelius and his friends are listening to the Gospel when the Holy Spirit comes upon them with external evidence, which Peter and the other Jews recognize.

Acts 10:44-48 *"While Peter was still speaking these words, the Holy Spirit came on all who heard the message. The circumcised believers who had come with Peter were astonished that the gift of the Holy Spirit had been poured out even on the Gentiles. For they heard them speaking in tongues and praising God.*

Then Peter said, "Can anyone keep these people from being baptized with water? They have received the Holy Spirit just as we have"? So he ordered that they be baptized in the name of Jesus Christ. Then they asked Peter to stay with them for a few days." NIV

Since we cannot see the internal living water, we cannot be sure, but it appears that in both the last two cases the second measure was poured out simultaneously, if not before, the first measure. At any rate it is clear that there are indeed two separate measures, one to eternal life, the other an outpouring that can be seen by observers.

THE ARGUMENT

The main point of contention comes from two groups. The first group, having received the first measure of the Holy Spirit, knows they are "saved." They have eternal life and a relationship with a living God in and through Jesus Christ and the presence of the Holy Spirit. The second group, having received the very evident second measure, assumes that since they did not have such an exciting experience before, that this second measure is **the** measure. Or they assume that since their "first measure" friends have not had this exciting manifestation of the Holy Spirit, that the friends do not have the Holy Spirit.

In practice, the "first group" often looks at the second and does not feel from nor see in them Christian love, and rejects their beliefs and practices as non-Christian. The "second group" often looks at the first and rejects them as non-Christian because they do not evidence the power. The first group often accuses the second of unscriptural behavior (often true, if it is without love), and the second group accuses the first of not having the Holy Spirit, and in extreme cases, of not even being Christian (not true on either count, as they are born again by the Holy Spirit). It is interesting that the ones who "have the most," that is, they have both measures, are the ones who are most usually wrong in their assumptions and accusations against the other. **It is not what we believe in that seems to cause the problem, but that we deny the others' beliefs as valid.** We disregard the basic instruction about the Body of Christ, and we say "because you are not like me I don't need you," or "because you are not like me we are not part of the same body." 1 Corinthians 12 says that is not acceptable Christian behavior.

A worthwhile time might be dedicated to intense study of the following scripture selections that will prepare us for a healthier understanding of the conflict, while also equipping us with the Biblical tools that are helpful in sharing both measures with others.

SCRIPTURES:

Acts 2:37-39	Salvation requirements
Romans 10:8-10	Salvation requirements
John 4:13-14	First measure - to eternal life
John 7:38-39	Second measure - rivers flowing out
Acts 8:12-17	Scriptural verification in fact
Acts 1:8	Purpose of Power
Mark 16:20	Purpose of Power
Matt 28: 18-20	Purpose of Power
Mark 16:15-18	Manifestation of Power
1 Cor 12:8-10	Manifestation of Power

Acts 10:44-46   Manifestation of Power
Acts 4:8   Manifestation of Power
Acts 4:29-31   Manifestation of Power
1 Cor 12:31   Request the gifts

NECESSITY OF BEING "FILLED" [BAPTIZED] BY THE SPIRIT

Compare John 3:16 with Luke 3:16 Salvation and Empowerment
Consider John 7:37-39 out flowing
Consider John 1:33 as pertaining to the unique ministry of Jesus
Acts 1:5,8 promise to the early Church
Acts 8:14-17 the need as the Apostles saw for believers

LITERAL CONFUSION

Confusion does come from the term Spirit filled, because even the Bible seems to use the term in conflicting ways. Equal confusion comes when the term "baptized" is used in reference to receiving the Holy Spirit. It is a perfectly good word because Jesus used it, but sometimes, in order to avoid the confusion, we use the term "empower" rather than baptize.

John the Baptist is described as being filled with the Spirit:
Luke 1:15,16 *"For he shall be great in the sight of the Lord, and shall drink neither wine nor strong drink; and he shall be filled with the Holy Ghost, even from his mother's womb. And many of the children of Israel shall he turn to the Lord their God."* NIV

John's father was also Spirit filled:
Luke 1:67-68 *"And his father Zacharias was filled with the Holy Ghost, and prophesied, saying, Blessed be the Lord God of Israel; for he hath visited and redeemed his people."* NIV

Obviously, this is not the same filling as to eternal life, for neither John or his father could have received everlasting life through Jesus' death and resurrection yet.

Another confusion comes from the fact that we seem to need continual refilling, since the containers are leaky earthen vessels. In Acts, the Christians are repeatedly "filled with the Spirit."

Initial Filling for Peter and others
Acts 2:4 *"All of them were filled with the Holy Spirit and began to speak in other tongues as the Spirit enabled them."* NIV

Refilling
Acts 4:8 *"Then Peter, filled with the Holy Spirit, said to them: >Rulers and elders of the people!"* NIV

Acts 4:31 *"After they prayed, the place where they were meeting was shaken. And they were all filled with the Holy Spirit and spoke the word of God boldly."* NIV

Acts 13:52 *"And the disciples were filled with joy and with the Holy Spirit."* NIV

Initial Filling for Paul
Acts 9:17 *"Then Ananias went to the house and entered it. Placing his hands on Saul, he said, Brother Saul, the Lord Jesus, who appeared to you on the road as you were*

coming here--has sent me so that you may see again and be filled with the Holy Spirit." NIV

Refilling for Paul
Acts 13:9 *"Then Saul, who was also called Paul, filled with the Holy Spirit, looked straight at Elymas and said..".* NIV

ARGUMENT AGAINST BAPTISM with HOLY SPIRIT

In one seminar for pastors, the head of a Bible School, with a Doctorate in Theology, made the comment during a break that the 1 Corinthians 12 gifts are no longer operating today. I (Hugh Kaiser) asked why he thought so, and he led us to 1 Cor 13:8-12.

8 Charity never faileth: but whether there be prophecies, they shall fail; whether there be tongues, they shall cease; whether there be knowledge, it shall vanish away.
9 For we know in part, and we prophesy in part.
10 But when that which is perfect is come, then that which is in part shall be done away.
11 When I was a child, I spake as a child, I understood as a child, I thought as a child: but when I became a man, I put away childish things.
12 For now we see through a glass, darkly; but then face to face: now I know in part; but then shall I know even as also I am known.
13 And now abideth faith, hope, charity, these three; but the greatest of these is charity.

He explained:
"When Paul wrote this letter, we did not have our Bible. It was only later that the Bible, which we consider

114

as the perfect Word of God, came to us. When the Bible came, that perfect thing came, and with it the cessation of these supernatural gifts. No longer needed, since we have the perfect Word, the Bible."

I agreed with him on the statements about the Bible both not being in existence at the time of Paul writing, and perfect, coming since that writing.

"The Charismatics and Pentecostals say the 'that which is perfect' is the second coming of Christ, but that could not be, because the Greek word for 'that which is perfect' is neuter, and Christ is always referred to as masculine in the Greek."

I had to defer to him as a scholar and I accept his explanation of why 'that which is perfect' cannot refer to Christ.

Then I had some questions for him:

The writing refers to a time as 'now,' that is, when Paul wrote the letter, and 'then,' that is the time when 'that which is perfect' has come. He agreed with me.

According to this passage, when the 'then' has come, we will see face to face. I take this to mean we will see Jesus face to face at the 'then' time. He agreed with my interpretation.

I remarked that I have never met anyone who claims to have met Jesus face to face in the manner of this verse. He acknowledged that neither he nor anyone he knew had met face to face with Jesus.

Again, when 'then' has come, we will know even as we are known. I take this to mean we will know Jesus even as he knows us. The good Doctor of Theology agreed with this interpretation.

We also agreed that no one in our group had ever met anyone who claimed to know Jesus as well as Jesus knows us.

Therefore, I conclude that the 'then' could not have come yet, and could not refer to the Bible, the perfect thing that indeed did come after Paul and before now, and that since the 'then' has not come, then there is no scriptural evidence that these gifts should have ceased in the church.

He could not find fault in my argument, but still could not agree that these supernatural gifts, which come with what Jesus called the Baptism with the Holy Spirit (Acts 1:5 and 1:8) could actually be in operation today. We agreed amicably to disagree, without argument.

(footnote to story: I heard a few months later the good Doctor of Theology had been excommunicated from his denomination for speaking in tongues).

In summary, **do not let semantics cause divisions and arguing in the church.** Love one another in Christ since we all have the Spirit, we are called to strive for unity in the Spirit. Don't let the three young ladies and their boy friends have a party in your Christian life! Above all, do not allow spiritual pride overtake you. Remember, whatever experience you have or have had with the Holy Spirit, it does not make you better than other Christians. **It only makes you better than you yourself once were!**

There are TWO MEASURES of the Holy Spirit available to believers. The first measure of the Holy Spirit given by Jesus is the in-filling that gives the believer a relationship with God; to **know** God and Jesus Christ. He defines eternal life as this relationship with the Father and Himself [John 17:3]. Only by the Holy Spirit's indwelling can this relationship be developed. On the first Resurrection evening, in the Upper Room, Jesus "breathes" on the disciples gathered [John 20:22] and said, "receive the Holy Spirit." This was their "first measure" or initial infilling that gave them "new birth." The Greek word, *"emphusao"* is found only in this verse, and in the Septuagint [Greek version of the Old Testament] at the Creation when God breathed into Adam and he became a living soul, and in Ezekiel's prophesying "breath" to the dry bones resulting in a restoration of a people. In each of the three examples, "new birth" results from the action of the Spirit [breath] of God. To the evangelical this "infilling" comes with acceptance of Jesus as Savior; to the sacramentalist it is accompanied in water baptism. The first emphasizes more the responsibility of man while the latter emphasizes the action of God. Both are correct! The problem comes when we "sacramentalize" and fail to "evangelize" people. The sacramentalist needs to provide opportunity for the person to actualize in their life the reality of this relationship with God and Jesus Christ through a personal acknowledgment of Jesus as Savior. The evangelical will do well to assist the believer in realizing GRACE is a gift from God, and salvation is not earned but is given through the merits of Jesus Christ.

But there is still more for the first disciples, and likewise for us, and He gives the second measure on Pentecost. The first measure was to give them **new birth;**

117

to make them a new people. The second measure was to give them **power for witnessing and ministry.**

The second measure of the Holy Spirit given by Jesus is an "out-flowing" that **empowers** the believer to share that relationship he has with God and Jesus Christ with others. The ability to witness to the relationship a believer has with God and Jesus Christ was the explanation given by Jesus for the gift of the Holy Spirit on Pentecost [Acts 1: 5, 8]. This measure is commonly called "the Baptism in the Holy Spirit."

HOW TO RECEIVE THE BAPTISM IN THE SPIRIT!

We suggest the following steps in leading a person into receiving the Baptism in the Holy Spirit [Acts 1: 5, 8; Acts 8:14-17; Luke 3:16]. Manifestations such as tongues **may** occur, and the person should be encouraged to expect an accompanying manifestation. In every scriptural instance of the work of the Holy Spirit, manifestations accompanied His action.

The person desiring to receive the Baptism in the Holy Spirit is to:

1. Renounce occult practices; confess unrepentant sins; ask forgiveness

2. Accept Jesus, or renew commitment to Jesus as Savior

3. Ask Jesus to baptize [immerse, empower] with the Holy Spirit.

4. Pray with the person using both vernacular and personal prayer language. Encourage the release of the Holy Spirit in their own prayer language, but do not belabor the issue lest it appears that you are more interested in their speaking in tongues than experiencing the Holy Spirit in whatever way He touches the person's life. Tongues are important, but the manifestation may not appear until later. And there may be other manifestations.

Remember, one receives the Baptism in the Holy Spirit the same way one receives Jesus in Salvation - **by faith**! See Luke 11: 11-13.

SPIRITUAL GIFTS

One evening I [Hugh Kaiser] was waiting for friends to pick me up for a meeting. I had about ten minutes to wait, and picked up my Bible. "Teach me something new," I asked the Lord.

I opened to 2 Chronicles 25:5-15 (Selected parts here): *"Amaziah called the people of Judah together and assigned them according to their families to commanders of thousands and commanders of hundreds for all Judah and Benjamin. He then mustered those twenty years old or more and found that there were three hundred thousand men ready for military service, able to handle the spear and shield. . . . When Amaziah returned from slaughtering the Edomites, he brought back the gods of the people of Seir. He set them up as his own gods, bowed down to them and burned sacrifices to them. The anger of the LORD burned against Amaziah, and he sent a prophet to him, who said, "Why do you consult this people's gods, which could not save their own people from your hand?"* NIV

After reading this passage, I told the Lord, "This is a very interesting story, Lord. What is its meaning for me tonight?" The Lord replied, "You are like King Amaziah. I give you victory over the enemy through powerful gifts of the Spirit. After the victory, you set the gift, or the method, up as your idol, thinking that it is the gift, or the method that gave you victory. You forget where the power and victory really come from: the Lord your God."

This lesson has come up time and time again as I travel and minister. Sometimes it comes up as pride when I watch someone else minister and think I have a "better" way. Sometimes it comes up as frustration when my method does not produce the expected results. Sometimes it comes up as the Lord leads me to do something foolish and I resist.

Foolishness

One time a friend asked me to pray for his injured knee. As I knelt praying, I had the thought I should hit the injured knee. I thought, "This is foolishness. The knee is already injured. Hitting it will make it worse." The thought would not go away, so I considered it might be from the Lord, and began to consider the action. I thought I might just tap the knee a little, and the thought came into my mind of the time Joash was told to take arrows and strike them (2 Kings 13:18-19). He did not receive total victory because he only struck the arrows three times. Finally I decided to hit the knee, much to the surprise of my friend. Even more surprising to both of us, is that when I hit him, he was healed.

The point is that while we can study the gifts for understanding, we will never fully understand. While we can use the gifts for service and ministry, we do not control gifts.

The Lord wants to control us in our use of the gifts, in their administration and operation. We cannot judge by appearance others' use of gifts, nor should we think gifts are so special they are to be idolized as the source of power. God wants us to follow Him, not our methods or doctrines, religion, or gifts. We need to walk in the Spirit, not with our own sight and understanding. With this understanding and attitude, we can begin to look at the gifts.

GIFTS IN THE BIBLE

Spiritual gifts are listed in four major places in the New Testament: Romans 12: 6-8, 1 Corinthians 12: 8-10, 1 Corinthians 12: 28 and Ephesians 4:11. Ephesians 4 contains a list of types of leaders given to the church by Jesus, and is presented earlier. The others are examples of gifts brought by the Holy Spirit in doing His work among us: comforting, guiding, teaching, leading to Christ, and providing demonstration of God's power in the Gospel.

Gifts are used in ministry to others hence they are included in this section on ministry. How and when these gifts are exercised can reflect maturity, but their presence or absence is not related to spiritual maturity.

Whenever we talk about gifts of the Spirit, we should remember that in the Bible each time gifts are taught, more space is devoted to teaching about love and unity of the body of Christ than about the gifts. The gifts are to flow from unity and love to be truly effective for the Kingdom of God. It is also apparent that different people or groups will have different gifts, and that the gifts will be administered and operate differently. This accounts for valid differences between groups of Christians. It also accounts for jealousy and arguments between groups of Christians, though as we have already seen, this is not a valid excuse for such divisive behavior.

We saw in our study of Ephesians 4:11-12 that the body of Christ will grow when the people of God exercise the gifts in ministry, but the requirements for this growth include love and unity as well as activity. Now we will focus on the gifts and operation, but keep in mind that this is but one of a trinity of requirements.

Romans 12:6-8 includes prophecy, ministry, teaching, exhortation, giving, leading, and mercy.

1 Corinthians 12:8-10 contains nine "supernatural" gifts. These are gifts that operate outside of natural laws. We will focus on these since they cause division and misunderstanding between Christian groups. At the end of chapter 12, apostles, prophets, and teachers are added to this list. These are included in the gifts of leaders given by Jesus listed in Ephesians 4.

The Corinthian Gifts
The list of nine is not all-inclusive, but contains the most abused and misunderstood of the gifts among the Corinthians, and represents the least understood and most divisive gifts in the body of Christ today. Another gift in the same category is in Mark 16:17 that being the casting out evil spirits. Certainly there are many other gifts, administrations and operations.

The Corinthian letter was written primarily to correct problems in this church. It is a letter of corrections. The Corinthians had every spiritual gift operating among them, yet they were spiritual babies. From chapters 12-14 we can see that the Corinthians needed correction in the operation of the gifts in the congregation.

Paul's Introduction
Paul teaches about the gifts in chapter 12, as he explains:
v1 *"Now about spiritual gifts, brothers, I do not want you to be ignorant."* NIV
v4 *"There are different kinds of gifts, but the same Spirit."* NIV

v5 *"There are different kinds of service, but the same Lord."* NIV
v6 *"There are different kinds of working, but the same God works all of them in all men."* NIV

v 4: different gifts.   Same Spirit
v 5: different ministries   Same Lord
v 6: different works   Same God
Notice in the right hand column we have the Trinity.

God is doing a work in and through us. The Lord Jesus gives us each a ministry to accomplish this work. As we do the ministry the Lord gives us, the Spirit flows from us with power, evidenced by what we call gifts.

Different Gifts
You and I may have different gifts. I have gifts of healing (sometimes, but not usually miraculous). You may have gifts of miracles and I might get jealous because you attract attention, and it seems like your gifts are better than mine. I may not even discover my gifts because I am too busy wishing I could be like you! Paul says don't worry, each one has different gifts, but it is the same Spirit!

Different Ministries
Maybe we have the same gift. Many people know of Benny Hinn and see him as having gifts of healing. I also have gifts of healing. But the ministry I have is far different from that given to Hinn. For one thing, he ministers to thousands, and is famous. I minister to small groups, and few know about me! His ministry is quite flamboyant, throwing coats, blowing, and waving his arm. When he does this, the power is awesome! My ministry is very quiet. I hardly touch people when I pray, and while the power is frequently exhibited in similar ways, it takes

me a long time to pray for one person. I pray for the people individually, he prays for groups. It is a different ministry, though many of the same gifts are in operation. I could wish (and sometimes when I am in the flesh, do) that my ministry were more famous like his. But the Lord has given me the ministry I have, and I love it. I get to see into the people's lives, I get to know them. I can do this with small groups, but with thousands, forget it!

Mary was a gifted flower arranger, and arranged the flowers for every church service. She enjoyed the job, but thought that it would be nicer if someone could work with her. Besides, if another person were involved, she could take a vacation with her family sometimes. Judy, the wife of a funeral home director, started coming to their church. Judy was very gifted with flowers also, and did all the arrangements for funerals. Mary was more than disappointed when Judy refused to help her with the church service arrangements. She was angry. Judy had the talent, had the time, and absolutely would not help her!

In fact, Judy realized her ministry was for funerals, not for church services. This is what the Lord had called her to, and the Lord had not called her to work with Mary. Mary could not understand because she never thought of it in terms of what the Lord was calling Judy to do. Mary thought Judy was proud, and felt rejected and resentful. In actuality, each had been given a ministry and such thoughts and emotions were childish.

Different Works
Maybe we both have the same gifts and the same ministries. The working of God in these ministries through the gifts may be quite different. The working of one may be very noisy and aggressive, the other quiet and

unobtrusive. Also, we cannot always see the results of the ministry, the work that God is doing through us.

Ephesians 3:10 describes one of the purposes of the church: *"His intent was that now, through the church, the manifold wisdom of God should be made known to the rulers and authorities in the heavenly realms."* NIV

The work God is doing is visible to the spiritual realms, but not always to us. It is good to remember this when we feel discouraged!

Gifts

Everyone has a gift and a ministry, God works in each one! The power of the Spirit is manifest, or evident, in each one.

1 Cor 12:7 *"Now to each one the manifestation of the Spirit is given for the common good."* NIV

1 Cor 12:11 *"All these are the work of one and the same Spirit, and he gives them to each one, just as he determines".* NIV

v 7: given to each one, for the common good
v11: given by the same Spirit; given to each one;
      the Holy Spirit decides who gets what.

Does any part not have a gift? No, every part has a gift. We see another part of Misunderstanding Ministry here. We expect every part of the body to be like us. When it isn't, we complain that they really aren't in the same body. This is not new, for Paul addresses this issue, too.

Body Language

Once when attending a Church Conference, the speaker was speaking about a "hot" social issue and the church's responsibilities. I had sought the Lord and was convinced the Lord had led me in just the opposite direction as this person was promoting. As the judgment rose up in me against the other, the Spirit in me witnessed to the Spirit in the speaker. As I listened carefully, I realized that this position had been arrived at only through careful prayer.

"How can this be, Lord?" I asked. "How can it possibly be that you would tell one of us one thing, and something just the opposite to another?" It seemed impossible to me. I believed that if my understanding came from the Lord, one who had a different understanding could not have gotten it from the Lord.

As I listened, the Lord gave me a vision. It was as though I were a left foot. and I could see. All I could see was the right foot.

As I watched, I noticed that the right foot always stopped when I moved, and always moved when I stopped. It was **never** doing what I was doing! The only time both were stopped is when the body was not moving.

Then I saw a hand. As the body walked (I assume, I could only see the right foot and the hand) it moved in very strange directions and ways. It seemed to have no relationship at all to what we feet were doing. It was really crazy and useless!

Then, I saw another hand, which I understood was the hand of another person. This one was waving about

127

here and there and was in my sight totally unrelated and useless.

Just as the scene zooms away to reveal a larger area in the movies, so the vision zoomed out, and I saw the feet and hands, connected to their respective bodies now. They were on a stage, a ballet in progress.

"Only the choreographer knows," the Lord spoke to me.

Since that time I have had some difficulty in staying judgmental toward those whose ideas are different from mine! This judgment towards others is not unique to me, nor is it new. Paul dealt with the issue in Corinth by the example of a body. I can easily see how the Lord must have showed him this picture!

1 Cor 12:12 - 27:
"The body is a unit, though it is made up of many parts; and though all its parts are many, they form one body. So it is with Christ. For we were all baptized by one Spirit into one body, whether Jews or Greeks, slave or free, and we were all given the one Spirit to drink.

"Now the body is not made up of one part but of many. If the foot should say, "Because I am not a hand, I do not belong to the body," it would not for that reason cease to be part of the body. And if the ear should say, "Because I am not an eye, I do not belong to the body," it would not for that reason cease to be part of the body. If the whole body were an eye, where would the sense of hearing be? If the whole body were an ear, where would the sense of smell be? But in fact God has arranged the parts in the body, every one of them, just as he wanted them

128

to be. If they were all one part, where would the body be? As it is, there are many parts, but one body.

"The eye cannot say to the hand, "I don't need you!" And the head cannot say to the feet, "I don't need you!" On the contrary, those parts of the body that seem to be weaker are indispensable, and the parts that we think are less honorable we treat with special honor. And the parts that are unpreventable are treated with special modesty, while our presentable parts need no special treatment. But God has combined the members of the body and has given greater honor to the parts that lacked it, so that there should be no division in the body, but that its parts should have equal concern for each other. If one part suffers, every part suffers with it; if one part is honored, every part rejoices with it. Now you are the body of Christ, and each one of you is a part of it." NIV

The connection to the body is not by choice of the member. Verses 15, 16, and 18 clearly reveal that God places the members just as He desires! It is obvious from scripture that we do not choose. Yet, just as we divorce our spouses against God's will, we try to divorce each other, or try to pull ourselves out of the body He has placed us in. We do not want to put up with a bit of discomfort, or even worse, corrective criticism!

Unity would be served well if we understood that God calls us and puts us into the body where He wants, not where we want. This should be considered when choosing a church home. We should know that God puts us there. It will help us stay there and do our part when the going gets tough.

Paul makes it clear that there are many different parts with different appearances and functions. A body that is all eye would be a very strange body, and how could it hear? If it were only ear, how could it smell? This is a very practical lesson Paul is giving us.

Remember that this is a letter of correction, and Paul is teaching about gifts of the Spirit. Evidently, use of and pride in the gifts caused as much problem in Corinth as they do in the church today!

In thinking about the body of Christ, it serves us well if we also remember the requirements for membership. Our Bible study (Born Again) reveals only these:
Receive or Believe in Jesus
Repent
Confess with our mouth
Be baptized

If anyone has done these, how can we claim that he/she does not belong to the same body as we? Much as we might think they are unpreventable (Paul used that word, see it?) we cannot divorce them. God put us with them into His body!

SUPERNATURAL GIFTS

St Paul is our contributor to the understanding of the working of the Holy Spirit. He gives in four locations information on the ways in which the Holy Spirit works. The "gifts" or manifestations and ministry of the Spirit can be found in 1 Corinthians 12: 8-10; 1 Corinthians 12: 28;

Ephesians 4:11; and Romans 12: 6-8. Traditionally, the listing in 1 Corinthians 12: 8-10 have been considered as primary manifestations of the Spirit, and some duplication may be found in the other references.

REVELATION GIFTS
Wisdom, Knowledge, Discerning of spirits

POWER GIFTS
Healings, Miracles, Faith

VOCAL GIFT
Prophecy, Tongue, Interpretation of tongues

Wisdom is the supernatural ability to know what to do, what to say, how to do something, and arrived at by means other than rational logic. It is knowing what to do or say, and when to do or say it. Doing the right thing at the wrong time, or the wrong thing at the right time, can be harmful. Word of wisdom is knowing what to do or say, and when to do it or say it, for a special situation. It is planted in the mind by God. If you receive a word of knowledge, you should pray for the wisdom of what to do about it.

This manifestation will assist the believer in various ways. One way in which I [Philip Weeks] experienced this gift was through being given exactly the right words in answering a question presented me by some serious inquirers. I had never previously considered their question, and had no prepared or learned answer, but the Holy Spirit gave me the answer that satisfied them.

Knowledge is the ability to know something that has not been learned, told to you or arrived at by personal discovery. Often in praying with a person, a "thought" will

131

come into your mind that you did not know, and becomes the "key" to unlock the door that leads to the person's benefit. This is a "word of knowledge" given by the Holy Spirit. It is information planted in the mind by God. The word of knowledge is beyond what we have learned. Often it is literally a word, though it can also be knowledge of a situation or event in someone else's life. The gift operates frequently in counseling and other forms of problem solving, in healing or intercessory prayer.

One night a lady came to our meeting and requested prayer. I did not know her or anything about her, but as I prepared to pray for her, the Spirit put into my thoughts "ask her about Mary". When I did she jumped in shock, and wanted to know whom I had talked with. I assured her I had not talked with anyone, and she knew for a fact that I had never before met her. Mary was her neighbor who was widowed, and this lady who had asked for prayer, had a resentment against her because her husband frequently helped her with chores like grass cutting and house repairs. God wanted to deal with her jealousy.

Faith is the supernatural belief and trust that something is accomplished before it is made evident. "Faith is the substance of things hoped for, the evidence of things not seen" (Hebrews 11:1). As with knowledge and wisdom, every Christian has faith. We could not receive Jesus as Lord and Savior without it. We are all called to grow in our faith, and our faith grows in strength with our Christian maturity. This gift of faith is a certainty of something not seen which is planted by God **for a special situation.**

A deaf mute was brought to me in Rangoon. She had read in the Bible how Jesus had healed people in her situation, and she came in faith that He would do the same for her. He did!

Healing is being used by God to give wholeness to a person through prayer, the laying-on-of-hands, the anointing with oil, or through exorcism. This does not exclude medicine. How precious it is when one trained in the medical science consecrates that knowledge and skill to Almighty God, and under the anointing of the Holy Spirit brings healing to hurting people. Notice that this one says gifts (plural) of healing, meaning different kinds under different situations and requirements.

On the mission field we have seen every kind of healing, and to elaborate on them would take several books. Jesus is the Great Physician.

Miracles are the working of God's mighty power that may seem to be against nature but are actually in the **super**natural realm while we live in the ordinary natural realm. We may be part of something happening without realizing the uniqueness of the situation until after the fact, and then conclude that, "it was a miracle."

On my first trip into China as a Bible smuggler, we were told to meet our Chinese contact at a certain hotel. However, the only way in that year one could travel in China was to engage a taxi through an assigned person [like the concierge] in the hotel. My companion and I each had two large suitcases filled with Bibles. We had entered China as part of a tour group, and had been put in a hotel from which we did not have the liberty to transfer. Our contact was at another hotel. The only way to get there was by taxi, and we would be at a loss explaining to the taxi reservationist why we were going to another hotel with four suitcases, yet planning to come back to our hotel later.

Having been in prayer for more than an hour before leaving our room, we walked through the hotel lobby to the front entrance of the hotel. Almost immediately a taxi drove up. The driver opened the trunk. We looked and saw no one waiting for a taxi. In fact, the reservationist appeared to be asleep at his desk. We put the suitcases in the trunk. I handed the driver a note with the name of our destination written in Chinese. We successfully made the delivery, but when we tried to get a taxi to take us back to our hotel, no driver would permit us into his car until we applied to the concierge who then directed the driver. God had ordered our taxi. We were part of a miracle without realizing it until it was all over.

Discerning of spirits is the ability to distinguish between that which is from God and that which is from Satan. Angels come from God; demons come from Satan. We are involved in spiritual warfare with powers and principalities unseen. It is necessary to be able to distinguish between these powers of the supernatural realm.

We had a Filipina dentist in our employment that every time evil was present got chill bumps. Like we receive a word of knowledge, often the Holy Spirit will put into our mind the awareness of the presence of an evil spirit.

Prophecy is to speak what God would say. 1 Corinthians 14:3 gives us a beautiful definition of prophecy as edifying a person, calling forth the best one has to offer, and strengthening the individual by the up building message from God.

Tongues are the ability to speak in languages not learned. The purposes for the gift are to (1) edify oneself through prayer and singing; (2) to pray intercession when you know not what words to pray; (3) give a message that requires interpretation; and, (4) may be used in exorcism [the casting out of demons from a possessed person]. This is probably the most controversial and division-causing of the manifestations or gifts of the Holy Spirit. Nearly every example of the power of the Holy Spirit coming upon people in the New Testament records speaking in tongues accompanying the event, leading some to believe it is the "proof" of receiving this power. However, if the other supernatural gifts are present, can we deny that these are just as valid manifestations of the presence of Holy Spirit power? They are all listed as equal manifestations in Corinthians.

My wife, who does not know any foreign languages, was part of a group praying for a young lady who said she had a problem but would not tell us the circumstances of her situation. As my wife prayed, she felt she should trust the Holy Spirit for the words, and began to "pray in tongues." The young lady grabbed her, saying, "How did you know?" She then explained that June was speaking perfect Spanish that the girl fluently spoke, and June was speaking directly to the problem and the secret circumstances.

Interpretation of tongues is to interpret a message spoken in tongues for the people to understand. It may or may not be a translation. Interpretation may also apply to dreams and visions.

One year we were unable to make contact with our Chinese counterpart and we were unable to deliver the

Bibles we had smuggled into China. I decided to go to the streets the night before our flight out to Hong Kong. We would give away the Bibles to any who would accept them. On our way to a particular street, we crossed a bridge that was over a street and walk way. A couple was walking below the bridge. I called out in Chinese and dropped over a Bible. They picked it up and asked for another, which I dropped. We went on to the selected street, distributed our Bibles, causing a mammoth traffic jam. Going back to the hotel, we crossed the same bridge, and now an old man was walking where the couple had been. I had one Bible in the pocket of my windbreaker. I dropped it over. He picked it up, and lifted his eyes heavenward. "Where have you been? What took you so long?" Four of us heard him. His English was perfectly free of accent. Was he speaking in tongues and his prayer language was English? Was he speaking in Chinese and we heard him in English? Was he speaking in tongues, and the interpretation was in English?

If you are sharing your experience with another, it is helpful if practical examples can be given as to how these manifestations or gifts operate in the Christian's life. They are very practical ways in which God strengthens the Christian and ministers through those who are receptive to the Power of the Holy Spirit. You may note ways in which these gifts have been experienced in your own life. When teaching this module, we often illustrate the gifts with actual examples of how we have seen the Holy Spirit work in these specific ways. The Spirit is always with us, and has greater desire than we understand to build us up as the Body of Christ. We have frequently received a "word of knowledge" when praying with a person, and pleasantly amazed, when sharing that word with the individual, how it opens the way for God to fulfill the prayer request in the person's life. We have experienced events that in human planning were totally impossible, but in God's planning appeared to us as "miraculous". We have heard words spoken by people completely unknowledgeable of a situation, yet the words spoke exactly to the matter. We have seen healings in almost every type of illness, and often immediately. We have laid hands on people with high fever and feel the break of the fever immediately. We have seen wounds heal overnight from the application of holy oil upon the wound. These are not manifestations of history, but contemporary actions of the Holy Spirit within the Church for the children of God.

In a seminar as well in your own private consideration now, it is helpful to note ways in which these manifestations may be "operational" in liturgical worship. There are acceptable places in the liturgy where singing in tongues, a message in tongues, interpretation and prophecy may be experienced, such as following the *Gloria in excelsis*, in the Season of Worship, or during the praise and worship following Communion. Anointing with oil and prayers for healing may be part of every celebration. Theologically, the anointing and praying ought to precede the reception of the Body and Blood of Jesus. Receiving the Body and Blood of Jesus is the ultimate medicine God has to give His people, and to hold a healing service **after** the Eucharist seems anti-climatic. A probable place in the liturgy would be after the Confession and prior to the Peace, or at the time when the people come to receive the Communion they go first to a station for healing and then to communion.

CONCLUSION

The "gifts" of the Spirit are really just the manifestation, or evidence, of the power of God flowing out of us to do the work of God as we obey his command and go into the world with His message. As with all spiritual things, our carnal mind is incapable of fully understanding the spiritual. We understand the best we can, and pray for God to guide us and correct us when we need correction.

The important thing is not who has which gift, or even how the gifts operate or what they are. The important thing is that each Christian understands that God wants to work in him. The Lord has a ministry to accomplish through him, and the Spirit will work through him with power. What we see when this power flows we call the gifts of the Spirit.

SPIRITUAL FRUIT!

It is an error to compare spiritual gifts to spiritual fruit. The person possessing spiritual gifts may not be mature as a Christian. St Paul, writing to the Corinthian Church [1 Cor 1:7] said they did not lack any gift; they were a very gifted church. But in chapter 3: 1-3 he calls them spiritual babes who had not yet grown to maturity but still acting in very self-centered ways. In other words, they were very gifted but their lives were immature.

Jesus also refers to those who were gifted [Matt 7: 21-23] to the point of prophesying and casting out demons, but they lacked in having a personal relationship with Him. He said the tree will bear fruit according to what the tree is like [Matt 7: 15-20], and by the fruit you will know the tree, not by the gifts.

THE GIFT TREE

In America at Christmas time we find a tree, cut it and bring it inside, put it on a stand and decorate it. We select and prepare gifts for each other, and place them under the tree. The gifts are distributed at a gathering. We do this for homes, office groups, churches, and other places where groups of people come together for work, play, or living.

Now let's consider a very important question:

What is the **RELATIONSHIP** between the **QUALITY** of the Tree and the **QUALITY** of the Gift?

If you need some help, the most common words used to describe quality are "good" and "bad". Is there any relationship between the quality of the tree and the quality of the gift? If so, what is that relationship?

Perhaps you (or your group) will need some extra help with this one. What determines the quality of the gift? Does the tree? Can a good tree have bad gifts, or a bad tree have good gifts?

In the shopping malls in America and many other countries, they have very large, beautifully decorated Christmas trees, with large, nicely wrapped packages underneath. The tree we see is beautiful and good. Do you think the gifts are also good? I don't. The nicely wrapped packages under those trees are all empty!

When I was young, we were quite poor, and could not afford to buy a nice Christmas tree and decorations. We cut our own tree from the forest, and made our own decorations. The tree was good for us, but for some who like the expensive decorations and tree, maybe it was not too good. The gifts were not wrapped so well (we saved our wrapping paper from year to year), but the gifts were terrific!

What determines the quality of the gift? For me it is the giver, and the love with which the gift is given. Do we come to agreement (hopefully, since I cannot talk with you to make sure you agree) that there is no relationship between the quality of the tree and the quality of the gift(s) underneath. A good tree can have bad gifts, or a bad tree can have good gifts.

We can draw a similar spiritual parallel as Jesus did with the fruit tree. The presence (or absence) of gifts, their number, or quality, has no relationship to the spiritual maturity of the person with whom the gift is found. We all know people who are quite spiritually immature who have some powerful spiritual gifts.

THE FRUIT TREE

Here we have a fruit tree.

You can choose what kind of fruit you would like it to be, but make it something quite familiar to you. In Asia the mango tree is the most common tree. Many people have mango trees in their yards, and mango is a common local fruit available in markets, so people know about it. In America it may be the citrus tree or the apple tree. For France, maybe it would be a grape vine, not a fruit tree, and in Germany it may be a cherry tree. Choose the kind of fruit to be something you are familiar with.

Consider the question.

What is the **RELATIONSHIP** between the **QUALITY** of the Tree and the **QUALITY** of the Fruit?

As before, if you need some help, the most common words used to describe quality are "good" and "bad". Is there any relationship between the quality of the tree and the quality of the fruit? If so, what is that relationship?

Do not read any further until you answer this question. If you are teaching this, do not go on until the class comes up with an answer. You may coach (does a good tree have good fruit? Bad fruit? Do you have a fruit tree? Is it a good tree or bad tree? How do you know?), but make sure they give an answer. Since it is a familiar thing to them, they should be able to answer the questions.

The group, when they start thinking about fruit trees, will come to realize that a good tree has good fruit, and a bad tree has bad fruit. That's how you know a good fruit tree or a bad fruit tree!

Does a bad tree ever have good fruit?

Does a good tree ever have bad fruit (note that the question is about bad fruit, not fruit that has been ruined or destroyed by outside forces).

If you (or your group) have any knowledge about fruit trees at all, the answers will be that a good tree cannot have bad fruit, and a bad tree cannot have good fruit.

We know that Jesus often used common examples to illustrate spiritual truths. In this case, the tree represents a person, and the fruit the spiritual character of the person. Is this a good spiritual truth, that a good tree (person) cannot have bad (spiritual) fruit, and a bad tree (person) cannot have good (spiritual) fruit?

If you think so, then I will ask you to show me scripturally, since we should never accept teaching without scriptural references. Where in the Bible can you find teaching about this?

Matthew 7:17-18. *"Likewise every good tree bears good fruit, but a bad tree bears bad fruit. A good tree cannot bear bad fruit, and a bad tree cannot bear good fruit."* NIV Now the questions get a bit more difficult.

Does a good tree **ALWAYS** bear good fruit (in the right season)?

This one you have to think carefully about. For example, in local markets (let's assume we made this a mango tree), are mangos always available in the mango season? Every group will finally answer "no" to this one, since some seasons are bad seasons. This does not mean the

143

trees are bad, but the season was bad. Sometimes, even a good tree does not produce good fruit in the right season.

If sometime good trees do not produce good fruit in the season, there must be some good reason. What can prevent a good tree from producing good fruit in the right season? Make a list. If you are teaching, make a list from the answers the class gives. What can prevent a good tree from bearing good fruit in the right season?

Here are some of the answers. In one class they had 15 different things (or lack of things), which can prevent a good tree from bearing good fruit in its season.

Note that some of these prevent fruit from being developed, some destroy fruit that is developing or already developed. The result is that we do not get good fruit from this good tree!

Here is another difficult question: Is the fruit that you find on a good tree always good fruit? This is tricky. The answer is "yes," though many will argue with you. When fruit is very young (green), for example, we consider it not good. The fruit is good; it is not yet ripe or developed. Green apples and green mangos are a delicacy for some people, so they would say that the fruit is already good just the way it is!

Another problem is fruit that has been damaged or destroyed. Some will say that the fruit is not good, and indeed, it is not good to eat. Yet the quality of the fruit is (was) good, it just was damaged.

The point here is that sometimes we think fruit is not good when we see in or try it, but maybe it is not yet

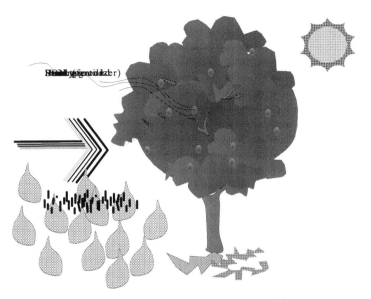

ripe. Or maybe it has been damaged, or something prevented the good fruit from developing.

In Asia, they have some very different fruits. Durien, for example, smells horrible, and for some people taste the same, but for some of us it is delicious. Rambutan (these two fruits carry these same names in nearly all countries) is another fruit with which you may not be familiar. Salak is found only in Indonesia. Peaches are found in the America. If you are not familiar with the fruit and the tree, can you pick good fruit? Maybe you have a hard time picking good fruit in the market (without tasting) even if you are familiar with it.

Often we have difficulty in determining if the fruit we see is really good fruit or not. Some fruit looks good but is not; some does not look so good but is actually delicious.

Come back to the lesson: Good Tree = Good Fruit; Bad Tree = Bad Fruit. But be careful in judging quickly.

Was Jesus talking about fruit trees when He told this story [Matt 7: 17-18]? No, we can see from verses 16 and 19 that he is talking about people and their spiritual character. When we consider the spiritual character of people, it is the Fruit of the Spirit, which shows us if they are good or bad, mature, or not.

We are admonished to judge, but we know from considering the tree that it is dangerous to judge quickly and that absence of good fruit does not necessarily mean that the character is bad. There may be reasons why the fruit is not there right now, or is damaged. This does not reflect the quality of the tree, or the true character of the person. This is why we should never give up on someone just because we think they are "rotten to the core". Jesus and the Holy Spirit can change people's character!

When we draw a tree that produces fruit [mango, orange, apple] we know that the quality of the fruit will depend upon the quality of the tree. If the tree is sick, the fruit will not be good. If the tree has fertilizer, water and sunshine, it will produce a good fruit. It is the same with the Christian. If the tree [our life] is filled with the Spirit and we grow in the Word of God and in our relationship with Jesus, the fruit we produce will witness to the effect Jesus is having upon our lives. The Corinthians had many gifts, but they were not mature Christians. They fought amongst themselves, and acted sometimes like non-Christian people. St Paul gives a list of those things that reflect the life lived apart from the control of the Holy Spirit in Galatians 5: 19-21. And in the next two verses he gives the list of things that the Holy Spirit will produce in the believer who strives to crucify their self-centeredness and fleshly desires.

We shall examine the Fruit of the Spirit.
FRUIT: Galatians 5:22-23
Love, Joy, Peace: Inherent characteristics of the Father given by the Spirit.

These three belong to the nature of God. God is love! The Joy of the Lord is my strength. The peace of God passes our understanding. The Spirit desires to work these characteristics of the Father into our lives.

Patience, Kindness, Goodness: Manifestations of the Spirit toward others. Jesus is patient with us. He is kind and went about doing well. He taught that we also are to do good even to those who do not like us. The Spirit desires to work these manifestations in our lives so our actions toward others will reflect the maturity of one who is learning to follow Jesus.

Faithfulness, Gentleness, Self-control: Manifestations of the Spirit toward God. Finally, the Holy Spirit desires to cause our spirit to respond to God with the same nature that portrays God to us. As He is faithful, so we are to be faithful. As He is gentle [meek in some translations] so we are to be a people not boastful, envious and confronting [vs. 26]. Placing ourselves under the control of the Spirit will enable us to live and walk by His direction [vs. 25].

Jesus said believers would be known by the fruit that follows them. People look at the Fruit of the Christian's life more than they observe their spiritual gifts. This is why

St Paul emphasized the importance of love. Without the fruit of love the gifts are overshadowed in the negative.

LOVE: There are three Greek words translated to the English word "love". English is a defective language in so far as its lack of various words expressive of the degree of meaning. We saw this in the "Born Again" module where English has only one word for "know" whereas other languages have a word meaning "informational knowledge", and a second word for "intimate knowledge". It is the same with "love".

In the Greek, "eros" is used for romantic and sensual love. "Phileo" is the word meaning "brotherly love". The love of which Jesus speaks and the love St Paul refers to in 1 Corinthians 13 is "agape". That is sacrificial love. It is the same Greek word St Paul uses as the fruit of the Spirit to be expressed in the Christian's life. Our love is to be self-giving.

Each fruit, as with the gifts of the Spirit, has its counterfeit. The counterfeit of love is **lust**.

JOY: Joy is the indwelling sensation given by the Holy Spirit that sustains the believer in the worst of situations. Jesus said He gives us His joy that no one can take from us. The counterfeit of joy is **happiness** because this feeling depends upon an external stimulant. Joy is given by the indwelling of the Spirit and is manifested regardless of the external motivation.

PEACE: Peace is the assurance the believer has from trust in God. Jesus says the Holy Spirit would witness to the teachings He gave, and this includes the many promises given in the Scriptures. God's peace cannot be understood

148

by the world because it is something only believers are able to receive. The counterfeit is **tranquility**, a false security produced by external stimuli.

PATIENCE: The only way we learn this fruit is in the midst of tribulations. It is the deep inner trust that all things work for the good. It is knowing that God is in complete control, and regardless of the circumstance, the outcome will be for the glory of God and the blessing of the Christian. The counterfeit is **tolerance**.

KINDNESS: When we are not self-centered, but have strong consideration for other people, willing to bear self-pain rather than cause hurt to the other person, you are expressing this fruit. Through kindness, the believer would prefer to hurt rather than in words or deed, say or do something that would inflict sorrow on another. The counterfeit is **flattery**, an untruthful, demeaning attitude.

GOODNESS: Goodness is caring to the point of personal sacrifice to bless others. To the Philippians St Paul said to consider others more esteemed than self, and this is the expression of goodness. The counterfeit is **bribery**.

FAITHFULNESS: This is a loyalty that does not betray the trust another places in the Christian. God is faithful whether we are or not. It is this same quality the Christian is to demonstrate. The counterfeit is **hypocrisy**.

GENTLENESS: If you realize you do not have all the answers to everything, and know there is still much for you to learn, you have then the spirit of gentleness. Some translations call this "meekness" which means to be teachable. It acknowledges each believer has something to contribute as the Spirit speaks through him or her. The counterfeit is **boastfulness**.

SELF-CONTROL: Our sins stem from our unwillingness to place ourselves under the control of the Holy Spirit. Our problems develop when we think we know better than God. Placing ourselves under the Spirit's control will reflect in our everyday behavior. The counterfeit is **pretense**.

St Paul says that against these there is no law [vs. 23]. They cannot be legislated. They develop as we rely more and more upon the Holy Spirit. It appears that Christians manifest much faster the gifts of the Spirit than the fruit. As in the natural, with a tree, it takes time to develop good fruit. Gifts may be more instantaneous. Do not be discouraged, or compare your life with that of another. The Holy Spirit does not take away our free will. He does exercise the right of conviction as the means of steering us in the proper direction, and He will work in your life the particular way you most need for him to change you. St Paul says the spirit of man is willing to yield to the Holy Spirit but our flesh sometimes is weak, and other times rebellious. It is when we fail to yield to the Holy Spirit that our fruit will be immature or rotten.

Primate Paulo Garcia - Brazil

Primate Loren Thomas Hines –Asia

CLARIFYING RITUAL AND LITURGY

In meeting with potential congregations inquiring about the Charismatic Episcopal Church we have found that one of the big issues is liturgy. Usually there has been misunderstanding about it, and sometime inaccurate teaching producing prejudice. In an attempt to clarify what liturgy is, and to correct errors of the past that have lead to negative reaction, we offer the following in the hope to produce a more healthy understanding of liturgy.

An "icon" is defined as anything [person, painting, statue] that represents something greater than the icon itself. When it is allowed to be a window through which the Greater it represents may be seen, it can be a wholesome aspect of the spiritual life. When the icon becomes so powerful that we see only the window and not through it, it can be destructive to spiritual development.

DANGER OF IDOLATRY:
Use of people as icons of God

There have been times in my own ministry [Philip Weeks] when I have admired charismatic leaders almost to the point of idolizing them. I am not a person who judges others in a condemning manner, recognizing that I have my own sins and lest I be judged, I should not judge others. This has in a way been a "gift" for me, because there have been times when I would idolize someone and Holy Spirit begins to show me "clay feet" of the person. I would always be surprised at what I was shown, and one time questioned Jesus why I was being shown frailties. The answer was very clear: "So you will not displace Me on the throne with that person".

It is easy for us to be enamored by the greatest of a fellow human being to the point that we give them more admiration than proper. Respect is to be given to our spiritual pastors whom God has put over us as authorities, but when we give honor to the extent that it goes beyond the realm of respect and into the realm of worship, it becomes idolatry.

Our leaders [Patriarch, Archbishops, Bishops, Priests] are men whom God has called for a special ministry, but nevertheless, men who have failings like all mankind.

Use of things as Icons of God

Use of things that cease to be icons of God and become objects of adoration; for example the Santo Niño, a statuette familiar in the Philippines of the Holy Child Jesus, and idolized, but when anything no longer exists as a symbol representing what the symbol is suppose to represent. That object, whether person or article, becomes the god by virtue of the position it is given. Such warps liturgical worship toward idolatry and spiritualism. There is an extremely fine line between adoration, respect, and given more honor than is suppose to be given.

154

A Thin Line Separates Magic and Mystery

MYSTERY	DANGER	MAGIC
Instruction and Power from God	We work as partners, God works through us.	Instruction from man Power from Satan
Work of the people	Leaders Required	One person, usually "outsider"
Language of the people	Special Language gives special meaning	Unknown language – "hocus pocus"
Open knowledge available to all	Training Required	Special knowledge
Free, open access	Training costs	For sale, secret
Allow God to work	Called to Action	Make something happen
Icons, Images, Pictures, Statues	Reminders are useful	Magic Charms, Idols

Abuses:
1. Idolatry - worshiping any of the pieces of liturgy
Altar furniture
Cross - icon - painting - statue
Clergy

Non-liturgical churches place the Bible as supreme symbolized by the centrality of the pulpit. Aglipayans and Roman Catholics adorn their churches with all types of statues and through misguided teaching have members who attempt to satisfy their spiritual need simply by crossing themselves when passing a church building, or seek protection in stroking a statue or relic of a saint. When over-emphasis is made about any object, regardless of theological persuasion, idolatry occurs. There is equal danger of making the object an idol by over-criticism, and through the negative ascribe to the object a status greater than that intended by those who created it.

2. Aestheticism - pleasing to the eye. A good icon is a window thru which one can see God but if the concentration is on the icon you don't see God.

3. Superstition - putting one's trust [Faith] in the image rather than the One it is to portray. An example is the priest rubbing the Santo Niño on the sick child as if the image contained miraculous powers, or the occult blessing of structures with use of chicken blood, going to witch doctor or wearing an amulet for protection. These are not of God.

4. Allegorization forces a wrong meaning or limit the meaning of a symbol to one thing because the mystery of God is greater; i.e. altar candles as two natures of God; Light of the world, etc. when there is also a very practical

purpose behind the symbol. Prior to "liturgical renewal" traditional churches placed an extra set of Eucharistic candles on the altar for the bishop's visitation. Some may still follow this practice. They became known as the "bishop's candles", and symbolized the bishop's presence, but the practical reason behind it goes back to a time when lighting was poor in the church, bishops were old and had difficulty seeing the missal, so extra candles were placed on the altar to aid the bishop in his reading the service book.

5. Magic versus Mystery - Magic is use of Satan's power rather than God's to achieve a purpose. The Christian mystery is our relationship with God and sharing His power through the blood (death and resurrection) of Jesus Christ (Eph 2:1-5). With magic you usually have an outsider who is the central figure in whatever is going on; with our mystery we have the priest, but Christ became one of us to accomplish the work, and our liturgy is the work of all the people to celebrate this event, and no one thing takes precedence over another.

In magic you often have relatively brief formulas not understood like "abracadabra or presto change" versus mystery which will be composed of relatively complex ideas but in language you understand.

Example: The Protestant Reformation attacked the Roman Catholic priest who spoke in a different language from the ordinary, and the people didn't understand. In good liturgy you have all types and kinds of people ministering: choir, priest, deacons, historical prayer, et cetera. People have their parts in responses. Without the participation of the people, the worship can be either entertaining or a magical event.

We must be careful not to hold up the leader to the point he is worshiped. The leader is present for a peculiar [special] function and nothing more. One has to be aware what you say about something and how you act about it, because over time the distinction may get lost. Worship is assigning "Worth To". Liturgy is to assign "worth" to God and sanctify humans as we are all set apart from God. If the bishop is the icon of God and you award him big things, the danger is this person is more worthy of being in that position than the ordinary unsophisticated person in the pew is able to tell the difference. Are we seeing the WINDOW or are we seeing THROUGH the window?

Sometimes our worship language becomes so special to us that outsiders cannot understand what we are doing or saying. We have embraced the magical practice of excluding non-members.

Are our offerings an attempt to respond to needs or a means by which to buy divine favors? Is wearing a cross intended to witness to our redemption, or as a protection against evil?

How do we discern the call of God? Do we choose only certain people like the handsome or the tallest, et cetera? We must be careful with vestments, houses, and decorations so as not to become enamored by the window, failing what is to be seen through it.

Is the Rosary a true guide in devotion, or is it something that we do in order to buy God's blessing? Are our offerings an attempt to respond to needs, obedience, or a means by which to buy divine favors? Is a cross worn to witness to our redemption, or as a protection against evil?

158

There has to be a balance between the meaning of the symbol and the value we attach to it, and a balance in the understanding of the meaning – Christ's representative includes servant, prophet, and caregiver of souls. The objects we use for devotion or witness must not have such value attached to them that they become the focus of worship rather than an aid. Never forget the definition of **SACRAMENT**: "an outward and visible sign of an inward and spiritual grace, given by Christ as sure and certain means by which we receive that grace."

Philippine Bishops with the Patriarch - 2011

THE SACRAMENTS

A sacrament is defined as "an outward and visible sign of an inward and spiritual grace, given by Christ as sure and certain means by which we receive that grace." [BCP] There are seven sacraments defined by the historical councils of the Church. Baptism and the Holy Communion are named as major sacraments. Confirmation, Penance, Unction, Marriage, and Ordination are called "minor sacraments" and not considered necessary for all believers in the same way as Baptism and the Lord's Supper.

A study of these reveal that God uses very simple elements and ways by which He gives His Grace to His people.

The validity of a Sacrament is usually determined by the following considerations:
1. Minister
2. Element
3. Subject
4. Intent
5. Formula or words established by the Church

A. HOLY BAPTISM

Holy Baptism is the sacrament by which God adopts us as His children and makes us members of Christ's Body, the Church, and inheritors of the Kingdom of God. [BCP] The Greek word translated "baptism" has several possible meanings. Out of Old Testament practice for purifying Gentiles, wishing to enter Jewish worship, the method of cleansing was through "sprinkling" or "pouring" on of water symbolic of washing. At the time of Jesus' earth ministry, Essenes practiced a baptism by immersion for purification and it was a repetitive act, sometimes as many as ten times a day. Every recognizable sin was repented of by an act of baptism. Both modes were prevalent in the time of Jesus' earth ministry. New Testament references to baptism imply both the mode of immersion, and affusion or pouring. Keeping in mind the definition of a sacrament, St Paul's teaching on baptism in Romans 6: 3-11 is clear that through this sacrament the former life is buried in Christ and a new relationship is given with God, and hence, becomes an icon to the world. As we are born in the flesh through water, so through water we are "born again" into the Kingdom of God. God is the Giver of that new relationship. Baptism is an initiatory rite that says to the world the baptized belongs to the God of our Lord Jesus Christ.

The New Testament is silent on the minimum age requirement for baptism, but considering initiatory rites from the Old Testament such as circumcision on the eight day to bring a male into Covenant with God, it may be concluded that young children were included in the baptismal rites of the Church, and especially can such be concluded when Paul baptized the Philippian jailer's household, and Peter baptized those in Cornelius' house. As in circumcision for the Jewish child, so in baptism we are brought into covenant with God. It is an action on God's part with man responding to His invitation to be His child.

In Baptism, the minister is normally an ordained person, however, in case of an emergency the Church permits any baptized person to administer the sacrament. The element is water; the person is one who has not been baptized; the intent is to make the person a child of God, a member of Christ's Body and an inheritor of the Kingdom of God; the formula is the use of the words "in the Name of the Father, and of the Son and of the Holy Spirit".

B. THE HOLY EUCHARIST

It has been said that the Eucharist needs no explanation to a true believer, and cannot be explained to a non-believer. Eucharist means thanksgiving; to give thanks. It is one of several names used for the primary act of worship in the Church. Other names are The Lord's Supper, Holy Communion, the Mass, the Divine Liturgy. St Paul commends it as a means by which we are reminded of the sacrifice of Jesus. Jesus commands it to be done by His Church as a means to bring Him [*anamnesis*; the opposite of amnesia] into the fellowship of believers. John 6: 56; Luke 22: 19-20; 1 Cor 11: 23-26; 1 Cor 10: 16-18.

In order to understand the nature of this Sacrament and what God has given us through the New Covenant, we offer a comparative study of worship and offering as revealed under the Old Covenant to that which we see in Jesus Christ through the New Covenant.

I. OLD TESTAMENT OFFERINGS
A. **Propitiation**: Gifts, sacrifices, and Offerings that are equal to those presented to a King or other ruler when one seeks favors. Basically giving in order to get.
Number 19:1-10; Leviticus 9:15

B. **Tributes**: Bringing to God as King and Landlord the first fruits [first born] and tithe as a tax due.
Exodus 13:11-13; Exodus 34:19-20; Malachi 3:8

162

C. **Alimentation**: Feeding God with the choice portions of an offering that was the fat and the blood. In Leviticus [2: 17] man was forbidden to eat the fat or drink the blood. These belonged to God and were offered on the altar to Him. It was the belief of the Hebrew people, along with other ancient people, that the immortal quality of the gods was sustained by their eating special food, or imbibing special drink in heaven. We are familiar with the Greek "food of the gods –ambrosia'." When they were present on earth they likewise needed special sustenance, and for the Hebrews "life is in the blood".
     Exodus 29:38-42; Numbers 28:3

D. **Communal**: the ancients sought to forge or cement relations with God by sharing a meal with him.
     Exodus 18:12; Deut 12:7

E. **Expiation**: Purging of sin with sacrificial blood; any contact with impurity, either physical or moral, any infringement of traditional taboos and any violation of cultic laws, were regarded as contaminating the offender's essential self. This unclean condition from sin could be cleansed by the blood of sacrifice.
     Leviticus 4: 1-35

II. NEW TESTAMENT OFFERINGS
Jesus turns the Old Testament system on its head: the action is initiated from God, not from man:
A. Instead of Propitiation, it is **GRACE**. Before we even know to ask, God gives
     Romans 5:6-11

B. Instead of paying Tribute we are **MADE HEIRS**
     Romans 8:17; Galatians 3:29; Ephesians 3:6; Titus 3:7

C. Instead of Alimentation, God **FEEDS US** with His Body and Blood

  John 6:35; John 6:48; John 6:50-51; John 6:53-56; John 6:58; Matthew 26:28; Mark 14:22; Mark 14:24

D. Instead of inviting God to a communal meal, **HE INVITES US**

  Luke 22:7; Luke 22:19-20; 1 Cor 5:8; 1 Cor 10:16-17; 1 Cor 11:23-29

E. Instead of offering the blood of animals to God, Jesus **OFFERS HIS OWN BLOOD** for us

  Ephesians 1:7; Hebrews 9:11-15; 1 Peter 1:18-19; 1 John 1:7; Rev 1:5

  The Holy Eucharist is one sacrament repeated regularly because the Church believes God's people needs regular feeding of spiritual food. The elements used are bread and wine. In some places members of the congregation prepare the holy bread; in other places unleavened bread in the form of wafers are purchased and used. The meal comes out of the Old Testament Passover meal or the Seder as it is known today. Jesus ate this meal with His disciples the night prior to His crucifixion. He elevates it to a fulfillment in Himself. Wine is used because it was what Jesus used, and typifies purification and cleansing by the nature of the wine itself. Wounds were cleansed and sterilized by pouring wine upon the wound. Wine that becomes for us the Blood of Christ cleanses us of sin, and brings us into a living Covenant with Jesus [John 6: 48-56]. The minister of the Eucharist is one ordained as a priest. The subject or recipient of this sacrament is any baptized person who affirms the Real Presence of Jesus in the sacrament. The intent is to bring us into covenant with Jesus and all the Graces contained in receiving the Body

164

and Blood of Jesus. The formula is a prayer of consecration that includes the "Words of Institution" or words of Jesus declaring "this is my Body; this is my Blood", and an invocation to the Holy Spirit to sanctify the bread and wine that they may become for us the Body and Blood of Jesus Christ.

C. CONFIRMATION

When Deacon Philip evangelized Samaria and baptized those who believed, the Apostles in Jerusalem, upon hearing of his successful evangelistic mission, commissioned the Apostles [Bishop] Peter and John to go to Samaria that the new believers might receive the baptism [empowerment] of the Holy Spirit as had been given in Jerusalem on the day of Pentecost. This giving of the Holy Spirit was for the purpose of equipping the new believers with POWER for living their Christian life and ministering as the Body of Christ. Always manifestations accompanied the imparting of the Holy Spirit.

A reasonable interpretation of Scripture declares this Sacrament as an empowering by the Holy Spirit. The New Testament term is "baptism in the Holy Spirit". In water baptism, the believers receive the Holy Spirit for regeneration. Through Confirmation the believer receives the Holy Spirit for equipping for ministry; empowerment.

How does one explain the place of this sacrament for those who come into Convergence from the Pentecostal-charismatic church? They have already received the baptism in the Holy Spirit. Because of the importance of Apostolic Succession to the Charismatic Episcopal Church, the sacrament of Confirmation is "affirming" what Jesus has already given, and submitting to the historical manner employed by the Church for receiving the strengthening gift of the Holy Spirit. For one baptized as a child, Confirmation is accepting for oneself what was done in Baptism - an affirming of Jesus as one's personal Savior, and accepting the baptismal vows made on behalf of the child by the parents and/or god-parents, along with being baptized in the Holy Spirit.

The Minister is a Bishop in Apostolic Succession. The Subject is a baptized person. The Element is the Laying-on-of-Hands by the Bishop. The Intent is for the Confirmand to receive the empowerment of the Holy Spirit. The formula is a prayer that expresses the Intent. The Bishop may add additional prayers to the prescribed liturgical words, and may "pray in the Spirit" [tongues] for encouragement to the Confirmand to release their own spiritual prayer language.

D. HOLY UNCTION

Healing was very much part of the Gospel ministry. Jesus healed those who were sick and delivered those possessed by the devil. The early Church was involved in praying for the sick. Jesus sent His followers forth to heal the sick. This is the ministry of the Church today, and must be understood as a corporate support ministry with those who are trained and engaged in the healing arts such as doctors and nurses. Physicians have in recent years declared that patients upheld with prayer respond to treatment faster and more completely than those who are not. Believing that God is interested in the whole person, the church's ministry will never be seen in conflict with the healing professions.

Unction is the sacramental name given to the church's healing ministry because a primary element in this sacrament is oil. Oil is symbolic of the Holy Spirit. In the Old Testament oil was used in the anointing of Kings, Prophets and Priests. Exodus 30: 22-25 is a formula for anointing oil that is used in the ordination of priests and bishops just as Moses used it in the anointing of Aaron as the first in Israel's priesthood. It is normal to use regular olive oil in the anointing for healing. There is a medicinal quality in olive oil. Jesus tells how the Samaritan poured wine into the wounds of the beaten man on the Jericho road and after sterilizing the wound with wine, poured in oil for healing.

The minister of Unction is normally an ordained person, however, the Church today acknowledges that any Christian may pray for the sick and anoint with oil. Usually, the Bishop blesses the oil for that purpose. The subject is a person who is sick. The element is blessed olive oil. The intent is for God's grace to be released for healing and wholeness of spirit, soul and body. The formula is prayer unto God on behalf of the sick. Some may invoke the Holy Trinity. Others may anoint in the Name of Jesus.

Caution should be exercised in any healing ministry, but not inhibited because of abuses. This area of the church's life is often plagued by charlatans and occultists. Wise is the priest who trains lay people in praying for the sick, and offering healing opportunities regularly.

A HEALING PATTERN

We use the following as the basis for teaching and training church members for healing services. We find on the mission field the quickest way to get people involved with on-hands-ministry is to have healing services. It gives the novice missionary opportunity to quickly become involved in ministry while at the same time blesses the people who are in need of prayer. This has been the pattern that has worked best for Barnabas Ministries.

HEALING: HOW TO CONDUCT HEALING SERVICES AND PRAY FOR THE SICK

There are various patterns for conducting healing services. Barnabas Ministries has used healing services as a fast way of involving team members in on-hand ministry. Healing services are also imperative for meeting the needs of many people with whom we work. People are in need and respond to the offer of prayer. Hurting people need a healing Physician!

The following are Scriptures proposed for the purpose of informing you of the Scriptural basis for healing services, as well as to build your faith in the God who heals.

1. **Is Healing For Today?** EX 15:26; PS 107:20; IS 53:4-5; MK 1:40-41; MATT 8: 16-17; 1 PET 2:24; ACTS 10:38

2. **Who Can Heal?** JN 14:12; MK 16:17-18

3. **How Do You Heal?** (TOUCH, LAYING-ON-OF-HANDS, PRAYING, COMMAND) MK 1:40-42; MK 5:35-40; MK 7:32-35; MK 16:18; MK 11:24; MK 11:23; ACTS 3:6

4. **Anointing With Oil!** JAMES 5:14,15; MK 6:12,13

5. **Exorcism:** MK 16;17; MT 8:16; MT 10:8

6. **Getting People Involved In Their Healing:** MK 3:5; JN 5:8; JN 9:7

7. **Authority:** LK 10:19; MK 16:17-18; MT 18:20; 1 JN 4:4; RM 8:11

PRAYING FOR THE SICK
1. Have the sick person tell you their need but don't let them talk too long about it. If it is something that causes pain, determine if the person is presently in pain. This is important for the end of the prayer time.

2. Be still for the Spirit to reveal anything necessary.

3. If you get a "word of knowledge", or "discernment", act upon it. It may require some questioning of the person. Pray silently for wisdom.

4. If the person needs to confess, ask forgiveness, or pray, then allow it.

5. You pray to God voicing the need. PRAISE! Pray in tongues! Spend more time in AFFIRMING healing than sickness; Praising God rather than bemoaning the infirmity.

6. When you feel the Spirit telling you to stop, STOP!

7. Have the person do something that would reveal healing.

MINISTRY PREPARATION:
1. Have those who will be ministering come together prior to service for prayer and anointing.

2. When the time to begin the actual healing, the individual teams should again pray together.

3. If you feel the anointing has left, stop and pray together again. If you grow tired because of many people, stop and pray for the strength to be replenished.

4. At end of ministry, the teams should pray together: THANKS AND PRAISE, LEAVING THE PROBLEMS IN THE HANDS OF GOD, RE-FILLING OF SPIRIT; PROTECTION AGAINST THE ENEMY. This is an absolute!

RESTING IN THE SPIRIT:
Some people refer to this as being "slain in the Spirit". We prefer the term "resting." The following scriptures will assist in your understanding this experience.

ACTS 10:10; 9:4: JN 18:6; 2 CHRON 5:11 -14; REV 1:17

Do not look for it and do not judge the result of your prayer on whether or not a person rests. If you sense it beginning to happen, let it happen without further assistance from you. Those laying-on-hands should do nothing that might be interpreted as pushing the person so as to achieve one falling down.

E. PENANCE

"Confess your sins one to another" [James 5:16] was the early church's way of reconciling a person who had through grievous sin broken fellowship with the Body of Christ. As the church expanded, in order to prevent abuse through idle talk and gossip, the priest was chosen to represent the Church in hearing the confession, and represent God and the Church in pronouncing forgiveness of sin. Jesus commissioned the first Apostles, giving them authority to forgive and retain sins [Matt 16:19]. There are those who argue that the name of this sacrament should be "Confession" because that is actually what is being done in the Biblical definition. The sacrament is given the particular name "Penance" because after a confession is made, some kind of deed is assigned the repentant that are called "penance". It is not intended to be punitive, but healing. The penance may be applicable scriptures that will re-enforce God's forgiveness and reconciliation with God and the Church, and assist the penitent in not again committing those sins. Priests are forbidden through their ordination vows to ever reveal sins that are confessed.

The minister of this sacrament is one ordained as a priest. The subject is the sinner. The element is the confession of sin and declaration of desire for forgiveness, along with the assignment of some act of penance. The intent is to declare God's forgiveness for the purpose of reconciliation to God and the Church. The formula is prayer.

F. HOLY MATRIMONY

God declared in the Old Testament that His creation is perpetuated through the union of man and woman. The

Church hallows the life-long union of a man and woman in the Sacrament of Holy Matrimony as they make their vows before God and the Church, and receive the grace and blessing of God to help them fulfill their vows.

The minister of Holy Matrimony is normally a priest licensed or approved by the respective governmental agency that is in control of marriage laws. The subject is an unmarried man and unmarried woman. The element is the exchange of vows. The intent is to bless and sanctify this union as a life-long union for the purpose of support and love and the procreation of children. The formula is a ritual that sets forth the purpose of marriage, the vows and appropriate prayers.

G. HOLY ORDERS

God establishes order in His Church. Jesus chose certain men to be His disciples and gave to them authority. In the Historical Module we discussed Apostolic Succession as the model Jesus established for the Church. Ordination is the setting apart of men for spiritual leadership in the Body of Christ in the fashion and manner of the historical Church.

The first Order is **DEACON**. The deacon is a visible servant role. The second Order is **PRIEST,** who is given the authority to officiate over the sacraments, to lead liturgy, and to pronounce God's blessing. The third Order is **BISHOP,** who is the successor of the Apostles and given authority over the Church.

In Ordination, the minister is always a Bishop who ordains or consecrates others. A group of Bishops consecrates a new Bishop. A Bishop ordains or sets apart a

Priest or Deacon. The subject is a male who has not yet been ordained to the particular Order in which he is being ordained. The element is the Laying-On-Of-Hands by the Bishop. The intent is to set apart the ordinand for the particular function to which the Order of Ministry prescribes. The formula is the invocation of the Holy Spirit for the particular office and function to which the person is being ordained.

One is not to be elevated to any Order in the Church without prior examination. The Canons [Laws] of the Church govern the requirements for each Order, and specify the moral quality expected of the individual.

There are provisions made in the Church's Order for women having the call of God upon their lives, to be set apart as a deaconess or nun, neither of which are part of the traditional sacred Order of Ministers, but valid servants of the Church of Jesus Christ.

Consecration of Philip Edward Phlegar Weeks as
Bishop - August 24, 2002

The Nature of Symbols and Signs

Perhaps the worst contribution American missionaries and evangelists have made to the Church is the bad teaching that renounces anything symbolic. One would think from some of the teachings we hear, that the plainer something is, the more holy it is. Symbols that pre-date the Protestant Reformation, that go back to the very start of the Christian Way, and some that go even into the Old Testament, are renounced as unnecessary. Some teachers go even so far as to declare them pagan. I wonder what God would say today to these teachers as He said through Ezekiel in the verse that pierced the heart of Bishop Moats [22:26] about profaning holy things that have been part of our Faith and Practice for centuries..

It is amusing to say the least, that those who debunk the Old Testament as irrelevant to the Church since we have the New Testament, find it most helpful in extracting money from people by advocating strongly Old Testament teaching about tithing. God made it extremely clear that He wanted symbols in His Temple because they provide a lasting impression that words do not provide. There is a difference between images and symbols. One memory trick is association, and symbols assist us in remembering things far better than mere words.

One particular feature of the early Church was the use of signs and symbols in their worship. All the signs used today are rooted on the greatest physical sign of all: God becoming flesh in the person of Jesus Christ. God initiated these signs as a means of communicating His salvation to us - becoming one of us that we may be with Him. The whole Bible is full of the use of these signs - garden, sacrifices, sheep, blood, offerings, bread, wine, altar and other symbols. The earliest Christian symbol was the FISH, often used as a means of identification as a Christian.

Creative use of banners, liturgical dance, traditional and contemporary music can enhance the worship. While many things used in the church for worship may have symbolic significance, they also may have a very practical purpose. One must be mindful that bowing before the cross or the altar is not a worship of that which is visible, but an icon of that which it represents and directs our worship to God Himself. Any thing that is over emphasized creates the potential of becoming an idol and destroys what is primary. A symbol is designed to portray a deeper meaning than what the vision sees. At the other end of the spectrum is the thing that is done or used so long that no one remembers why we do it. These practices or objects become meaningless decorations. Most of our buildings have some sort of decoration for which we don't know the meaning, and we enjoy them for the decoration alone. Always know the purpose and reason for the things used and done in a worship service! Banners decorate a church but more so, send forth a visual message. The same is true with pictorial type stain glass windows. These help us worship through our sense of sight.

1. VESTMENTS AND MINISTERS
The use of vestments goes back to the time when God was setting up the priesthood in the nation of Israel - Exodus 38 and following. He instructed the priests who served in the temple to wear a particular attire. Their practical application was to detract from the human nature of the officiant, and exalt the divine nature of the One to whom worship was offered. The usage suggested the extraordinary holiness of the act being performed and stood

it apart from the ordinary. The vestments were icons through which holy things might be seen in the offering by the priest to God.

There are several reasons for vestments. One important reason is the covering of the person in the image of the office that he is fulfilling. The people are not watching personalities, but they are seeing the offices of the church at work. Ministers wear vestments as a symbol of God's righteousness covering their humanity and weaknesses. They serve to highlight their worthiness to serve as God's chosen vessel, not on the basis of their ability but on God's grace and mercy.

The bishop wears a pointed hat called mitre symbolizing the tongues of fire of the Holy Spirit upon the apostles on the day of Pentecost. The two pieces of cloth on the back of the mitre symbolize the Old and New Covenant or Testaments. He may carry a staff called a Crozier as a symbol of his office and pastoral function as the shepherd. He will wear a signet ring or a precious stone ring, symbolizing his authority and belonging to the apostolic band.

The priest will wear an alb, or a cassock and surplice with a stole. The stole represents the yoke of Christ and different colors correspond to different parts of the church year. This helps us visually to worship God for He desires us to worship Him completely. The deacon will also wear an alb, or cassock and surplice, but will wear his stole only over one shoulder because he has taken on only half the responsibility of ministry.

Other garments may be worn from time to time:

Chasuble: the garment of the Resurrected Christ worn by the Celebrant and put on as part of the preparation leading to the Great Thanksgiving.

Cope: a decorative coat worn by priests and bishops in procession.

Dalmatic: a garment similar to a chasuble but with sleeves, worn by deacons and sub-deacons serving at the altar as assistant ministers of the Eucharist.

Zucchetto: A skullcap worn by prelates, archdeacons and canons, and sometimes by priests.

Biretta: A hat worn in procession, and out-of-doors, in colors according to the dress code below.

Today the Church vestments [cassock, alb, robe] covers the human clothing of the officiant and leaders of worship, equalizing them before God in holy array and sets apart the worship as special, sacred and different from the ordinary routines of life as might be suggested in the opposite with the leaders appearing in regular street clothing.

CEC Dress Code for clergy:

Bishop: Roman Purple [magenta] clerical shirt, cassock, cincture, and zucchetto, gold cross with gold chain

Priest: Black shirt, silver cross with silver chain

Deacon: Gray shirt, silver or wood cross with cord or rope

Archdeacons and Canons: Black cassock with red stitching; black zucchetto with red stitching.

Liturgical Colors:

White = purity, holiness! Used on Christmas,
Christmastide, Epiphany, Ascension, Trinity
Sunday, Saints' Days, Transfiguration; normally
used for Baptisms, Funerals and Weddings
[If a Church lacks the financial resources to have
altar vestments in all four colors, it is appropriate to
use White at all Eucharistic services]

Violet, or Purple = royalty, penitential seasons such as
Advent, Lent, in the hearing of Confessions

Red = Church events, church anniversaries, Ordination,
Confirmation, martyrs, Pentecost, the Holy Spirit,
Season of Pentecost to Transfiguration
[Some liturgical calendars call for red during Holy
Week. The red is not the traditional shade as used
on Pentecost, but an oxblood red, A serious
question should be raised as to the relationship of
normal red used for martyrs, and if the same is used
for Holy Week. Jesus was NOT a martyr, but freely
gave His life. The traditional color for Holy Week is
Violet/Purple except White on Maundy-Thursday,
and black on Good Friday]

Green = Growth and missionary emphasis, Sundays after
Epiphany and Kingdomtide starting the Sunday
after the Transfiguration until Advent

Black = Good Friday

II. GESTURES AND PHYSICAL MOVEMENTS

Gestures [making the sign of the cross] and bodily
movements [bow, genuflect, kneel] play an important part
in liturgy and in the religious conduct of man. Such

behavior derives its meaning from its relationship to the Holy. Hand movements are widely used in ritual and liturgical actions; the touching of holy objects, materials or men is performed according to a code that precisely regulates these gestures and their accompanying prayers and blessings.

III. RITUAL - A prescribed customary that helps us to orderly ascribe worthiness to a God who is a God of Order and not of confusion. Ritual is any order whether formal Liturgy, or informal pattern of singing three songs, giving the Lord a clap offering, and singing more songs followed by prophecy, etc. Don Moen's ritual: "God is good" *Response:* "all the time". "All the time *Response:* "God is good!" is a charismatic ritual, but few would admit it. The same is true with "Praise the Lord" and expecting a response such as "Alleluia"!

IV. BREAD AND WINE
     In the Eucharist, or Holy Communion, bread and wine represent the Body and Blood of Christ. The bread broken and the wine poured out speak of His death upon the cross. As a symbol of spiritual nourishment, the same bread and wine become for us a heavenly meal. Offering them to God upon the Altar, praying over them the words of Jesus when He elevated the Passover Meal to a fulfilled meaning in His Body and Blood, and invoking the Holy Spirit to cause these elements to become for us the spiritual food and drink of everlasting life, we believe we partake of Christ himself, and share in His Sacrifice upon the Cross.

     BREAD is used in the Eucharist rather than crackers or cake, because the Bread is what Jesus spoke of when describing Himself as the Manna that feeds us to

179

complete satisfaction. He is the BREAD of Life come down from Heaven.

WINE is used as the beverage of the Eucharist because it is what Jesus used. Wine is an antiseptic to wounds just as the Blood of Christ cleanses us of the contamination of sin.

The BREAD and WINE are discerned to be for us the Body and Blood of Jesus, the spiritual food and drink of everlasting life, because He said "this is" rather than "this represents", and St Paul makes clear in his teaching that this Feast is a joining of human nature to the Divine nature of Jesus Christ. The word used and translated "in remembrance" is "*anamnesis*", which literally means an act by which one is brought into reality in the present. In other words, Jesus says that through The Lord's Supper we bring His Presence into reality and thus in our midst and in our lives. While we may not understand fully the import and significance of this mystery, Jesus said that our partaking of the Eucharistic meal unites the believer to Him and He to the believer, giving life to the recipient. "Lord, I am not worthy that you should come under my roof, but speak only the word, and I shall be whole." In some churches the "communion" is received by intinction; that is, dipping the host [bread] into the chalice. When the blood [wine] is drunk, approximately only a teaspoon full is consumed. When Jesus said "drink ye all of this" He did not mean each communicant was to consume the whole cup, but only a small amount consumed, thus leaving for ALL to have opportunity to commune.

V. THE CANDLES

The candles are symbols of the light of life, the light and illumination we receive whenever we gather as God's people. From the very beginning candles and lamps have played an important part in the order of worship in the Church as they remind us of Jesus who is the Light of the world. The two altar candles symbolize the two natures of Jesus - True Man; True God.

VI. THE CROSS

If there is anything that should be a universal symbol for all of Christianity, it should be the cross. It is the perpetual sign of our salvation and victory over sin and death. It stands for what God did in Christ. Its use in liturgy brings to us the attitude of total submission and obedience. Being the focal point of the Gospel drama, it is a constant reminder just as what the Apostle Paul experienced, "I have been crucified with Christ; it is no longer I who lives, but Christ now lives in me".

The cross comes in varying sizes and forms ranging from simple Latin cross to crucifixes. Usually when the cross is carried in procession, it is proper to acknowledge its passing by bowing the head, comparable to one's salute or covering the heart with hand when the flag passes in procession.

VII. INCENSE

The practical use of incense in the Temple was to camouflage the odors from the animals being sacrificed. Certain priests were especially assigned to offer the Incense offering, and the symbolic significance in Scripture refers to the prayers ascending in the way the smoke ascends. Its use in worship today has the same significance, and involves our sense of smell and sense of sight in total worship of God.

VIII. BELLS

The use of a bell or bells may be used during the Sanctus [Holy, Holy, Holy] and in the Prayer of Consecration of Bread and Wine, involving our sense of hearing in worship.

IX. THE CHURCH CALENDAR

The early Church set aside certain events like Easter, Lent, Christmas, as feasts and days to highlight the gospel message. All are based upon the life of Christ and the Christian's journey in that life. Beginning with the first Sunday of Advent and proceeding through all the Christian events in a year, enables the believer to live the full experience of Christ's life on earth, and the sacred commission given to the Church.

Symbols are an important part of our worship. Presentation of other symbols might be introduced to the participant, illustrating how our five senses may be incorporated in worship. At the same time, we must be careful that symbols do not become the means of idolatry.

CONCLUSION

In 1994, Canon Weeks and Hugh Kaiser met Father Loren Thomas Hines a month before he was consecrated a Bishop in the Charismatic Episcopal Church. Father Hines, as an Assembly of God minister, had begun a work in the Philippines called The International Christian Fellowship. He had been on a journey toward convergence, and learned about the Charismatic Episcopal Church being on the same journey. It was the Lord's leading to bring Hines into this communion, and subsequently his congregations throughout the Philippines and Europe. He was looking for someone who would help teach his clergy about liturgy and sacraments. They were already well trained in evangelism and the charismatic movement. We made a proposal which he accepted, and the following January (1995) Kaiser and Weeks conducted their first seminar with Bishop Hines' clergy in Manila.

As a guide to teaching about the Convergence Movement to Filipino evangelical and charismatic churches entering the Charismatic Episcopal Church, Barnabas Ministries, Incorporated [headed by then Canon Weeks as the Executive Director] developed a MANUAL by which seminars were taught. Canon Weeks and Mr. Hugh Kaiser were the main teachers of this Manual to these Filipino churches, both in the Philippines and in the Confederation of Filipino Churches in Europe. Whereas the MANUAL was more in outline form, the foregone is a more fully developed teaching from this MANUAL in story form, excluding the more personal stories told during the seminar classes.

Mr. Kaiser is an engineer, retired from the United States government in which position he was a management consultant and trainer. He has been Canon Weeks' associate since January 1985, and since 1995 has been full-time in missionary work in the Philippines and Indonesia. Much of his work is training pastors. He has successfully applied secular skills to understanding, and teaching the Christian gospel, and trains indigenous leaders in use of their skills for teaching their own. He makes his home in Honolulu, and Surabaya, Indonesia.

Canon Weeks is a priest in the Charismatic Episcopal Church with twenty-five years pastoral experience and eighteen years missionary experience. He is Executive Director of Barnabas Ministries, Incorporated. He founded this ministry September 1980. In 2002 he was consecrated in Uganda Auxiliary Bishop for the International Development Agency of the Charismatic Episcopal Church. He was for a time supervising Bishop in Rwanda, and raised up Emmanuel Ngirumpatse as Bishop.

He then served as supervising Bishop of Tanzania. There he was followed by Daudi Chidawali and Charles Sekelwa. Finally, he was supervising Bishop in Burundi from which he retired in 2005. He is now retired, and serves as Missions' Consultant to the Patriarch.

It is our desire that this presentation be shared with those who are inquirers into the Charismatic Episcopal Church, and may be translated into the language of the people as may be necessary. While copyrighted, it **may** be duplicated and copied, but **not** altered, revised or changed. As a way for us to know the extensiveness of its use, it would be courteous for us to be notified of any duplication or translation made, by writing us at 208 Leewood Drive, Lynchburg, Virginia 24503 or e-mail to bishopweeks@barnabas.us.

Non nobis, Domine, sed nomini tuo da gloriam! AMEN [Psalm 115: 1]

Appendix

Immersion Only?

By: Archbishop Craig W. Bates, Patriarch ICCEC

After posting an article on Baptism several have asked me to address the question of immersion. The real question, for some, is whether or not baptism by "infusion" (pouring) is a valid baptism. This has lead some well meaning Christians to consider a "second baptism" since they believe that their first baptism, usually as an infant (a concern I addressed in the previous article), is invalid. They would argue that one must be fully "immersed" or "dunked", i.e., their entire body including their head must go under the water.

The New Testament gives no specific directions on how to administer the sacrament of baptism, with the exception of using water. However, those who support the concept of fully "immersing" or "dunking" argue that the Greek word "baptizo" means just that. They argue that baptism reflects the symbolic significance of being "buried" and "raised" with Christ. (Romans 6.3-4)

As a Pastor, I have had the joy of baptizing several adults (all never having been previously baptized) in either the ocean, a river, or a swimming pool. It was a wonderful occasion and the symbolism was indeed powerful. I have also had the joy of being present at an Eastern Orthodox Rite of baptism where the child was fully "immersed" into the water (with the exception of the head upon which water was poured). Again there was a powerful symbol of the naked child being immersed and then dressed in the white gown of baptism symbolizing the new righteousness. But though these events were joyful and moving they are not arguments for eliminating the well-established practice of "pouring" or "sprinkling" as practiced by the vast majority of Christians.

It is true that the Greek word "baptizo" is often translated "immersion." In the story of Naaman, at the direction of the prophet, Naaman went to the Jordon and "dipped" himself seven times in the Jordon. The Greek word here, as translated in the Septuagint 2 Kings 5.14, is "baptizo". "Baptizo" is not always translated as "immersed" or "immersion." In other contexts the word is used to mean "to wash" or "to clean up before dinner." In Luke 11.38, Jesus has been invited to dine at the home of a Pharisee. The Pharisee was surprised that Jesus did not first wash ("baptizo") before dinner. Certainly this does not suggest that Jesus failed to totally or fully place himself under water (take a full bath) prior to dinner. Mark 7.3-4 states, the Pharisees "do not eat unless they wash (Greek word 'nipto') their hands, observing the tradition of the elders; and when they come from the market place, to do not eat unless they wash (Greek word 'baptiso')." So, we see in these two places that the word 'baptiso" can be translated not only as immersion but also as cleansing. In other places it is used for "ritual washing".

The word "baptize" or "baptisma" is often used in a metaphorical or figurative manner. In other words, there can be an event in a person's life that is figurative immersion as in the case where Jesus is speaking in Luke 12.50, "I have a baptism "baptisma" to be baptized "baptize" with; and how I am constrained until it is accomplished." In Mark 10.38, he asks his disciples "Are you able to drink the cup that I drink, and be baptized ("baptisma") in with the baptism ("baptizo") that I am baptized ("baptisma")." And, the in Mark 10.39, he tells them that discipleship will result in such a baptism ("baptisma"). This of course does not refer to a second "water baptism" but rather that Jesus will be "immersed" into the suffer of the cross for our redemption and that as followers of Christ we to will be required to "pick up our cross" (Luke 9.23)

Jesus tells his disciples that they shall be "baptized with the Holy Spirit" (Acts 1.5). In fact we read it Luke 24.49 and again in Acts 1.4, Jesus is insistent that they not leave Jerusalem but to wait for the promise of the Father – the baptism with the Holy Spirit. This of course fulfills what we read in Mark 1.8, John says, "I indeed baptized ("baptizo") with water, but He will baptize ("baptizo") with the Holy Spirit."

Does this mean they were "dunked" with the Holy Spirit? No, in Acts 2.17-18, 33) we see that the Holy Spirit was "poured" out on them. Later Peter tells us that the Spirit "fell" upon them. And, we read of other events where persons are "baptized with the Holy Spirit". Clearly the word "baptizo" is not limited to the concept of "dunking" but can also include a metaphorical "immersion" or in the case of the Holy Spirit a "pouring" or "falling upon." I would conclude, as have the vast majority of Christians throughout the centuries, that to limit the use of the word "baptizo" to always meaning "immersion", "full immersion under water", or "dunking" is at best an over simplification and more so limits the concept of new life or new birth that our God wants, by grace, to convey to us. The Christian community adopted the secular Greek word "baptizo" and gave it a far deeper theological meaning.

In fact, far before the Christian community adopted the word the Jews used it, particularly the Essene community, to signify a "ritual washing". We know that the Gentile converts to Judaism under went a "baptism" before being circumcised. John the Baptist practiced a "baptism of repentance" suggesting that the Jews were in much a need of "conversion" or "purification" as the Gentiles. The word Baptism or "baptizo" had a far deeper meaning than merely being "immersed" or "dunked." It carried with it the notions of conversion, repentance, as well as, initiation into the community of faith.

Jesus and the early Christian community took the word and drew even further theological implications – as we have seen a sharing in his life and sufferings as well as an empowerment to proclaim the Good News. To use the word only in it "secular" usage causes us to divert from the entire Christian usage of it. We must examine the use of the word "baptizo" as it is used in the Scriptures and in the life of the Church.

In this brief article, I do not want to address once again the issue of "faith" and "grace" in Baptism, but would refer you to the brief article I wrote on the practice of baptizing infants. Nor, do time or space permit me to address a complete theology of Baptism. I am merely trying to guide us through the mode of baptism, i.e. is "pouring" or "sprinkling" sufficient for a valid baptism.

Scriptures are clear that the outward act of baptism and an inward transformation go together. (John 3.5, Acts 2.38, Acts 19.2-3, Acts 22.16, Romans 6.3-4, Colossians 2.11-12; Titus 3.5; and 1 Peter 3.21).

The Scriptures also show us a connection between baptism and the work of the Holy Spirit. Peter, on the day of Pentecost states, "Repent, and be baptized every one of you in the name of Jesus Christ for the forgiveness of your sins, and you shall receive the gift of the Holy Spirit." (Acts 2.38) In Acts 10.44-47, we read of Gentiles receiving the Holy Spirit prior to baptism and Peter interprets this event in such a way as to advocate for their baptism – "Can anyone withhold the water for baptizing these people who have received the Holy Spirit just as we have?" If the Holy Spirit is "poured out", as Scripture shows, is this connection between "water baptism" and the receiving of the Holy Spirit an indication that "pouring" can also be related to the practice of baptism?

It is true that the practice of "full immersion" or "dunking" is a powerful symbolic act stressing the idea of death, burial, and resurrection. It is a strong argument for its practice in the Eastern Rite Churches both in Orthodoxy and Catholicism. But it is not a argument to suggest that baptism by pouring is invalid for does it not relate to the "pouring" of the Holy Spirit into our lives. It seems to me that "full immersion" or "pouring" both, convey the grace of new life, cleansing, empowering, and initiation that are given to us in baptism.

It is also necessary to look at the practice of the early Church in order to see how these first century believers applied the texts. The Didache, written around 70 A.D. – one of the earliest Christian writings outside of the New Testament – is a good glimpse into the life of the first generation Church. The Didache certainly does not hold the same authority of Scripture it does give us an understanding of the practices of the earliest Christians who were not only born again and filled with the Holy Spirit but faced the day to day challenges of persecution and possible martyrdom.

The Didache reads, "Concerning Baptism, baptize in this manner: Having said all these things beforehand, baptize in the name of the Father and of the Son and of the Holy Spirit in living water (that is, in running water, as in a river). If there is no living water; and if you are not able to use cold water, use warm. If you have neither, pour water three times upon the head in the name of the Father, Son, and Holy Spirit."

There are many other early writings that suggest that "full immersion" or "dunking" is not the only means of baptism. Hippolytus of Rome wrote in the Apostolic Tradition, 21, around 215 A.D., "If water is scarce, whether as a constant condition or on occasion, then use whatever water is available"☐Cornelius, Bishop of Rome, wrote in 251 A.D. in a Letter to Fabius of Antioch, regarding Novatian, who was about to die, "he received baptism in bed where he lay, by pouring."☐Cyprian in a Letter to a Certain Magnus 69:12, written around 255 A.D, wrote, no one should be "disturbed because the sick are poured upon or sprinkled when they receive the Lord's grace."☐Tertullian writing in 203 A.D in a document titled On Baptism states that baptism is done "with so great simplicity, without pomp, without any considerable novelty of preparation, and finally without cost, a man is baptized in water, and amid the utterance of some words, is sprinkled, and then rises again, not much (or not at all) the cleaner." Obviously Tertullian did not consider baptism by immersion as the only valid form of baptism.

Christian art also show us that baptism by full immersion was not the only valid form of baptism. We have many pieces of artwork for very early in the life of the Church and not one of them shows baptism by immersion rather they show baptism by pouring using water poured from a cup or a shell. Even if the candidate for baptism is depicted standing in a river they are shown having a cup or a shell of water being poured over their head. We have lots of tiles or mosaics found in ancient churches, cemeteries, or catacombs that depict baptism being administered by pouring. The archeological evidence is overwhelming that baptism was not restricted to "full immersion" or "dunking" as the only means of baptism.

We, of course know, that eventually "pouring" became the more normative way to administer baptism. The practice of "pouring" continues to be the acceptable practice of not only Roman Catholic, but the majority of the churches that came from the Reformation – Anglican, Lutheran, Presbyterian, and Reformed. Even the Puritans and their Congregationalist counterparts in America continued to practice baptism by "pouring".

Once again a small group of believers coming from the influence of Zwingli and the Anabaptists of the 16th and 17th century that conclude that baptism by "pouring" or "sprinkling" was invalid and they hence required their

193

followers to be "re-baptized" and to do so by "full immersion" or "dunking". The practice became common among the Revivalist of the 19th century in America and under those churches that grew out of the Revivalist movement has impacted other continents besides America. Are we to conclude that all the saints and believers who received baptism by "pouring" or "sprinkling" from the first century up till the time of Zwingli are not invalidly baptized? Can we conclude that so many of the saints and believers from the time of Zwingli until the present who were martyred or gave their lives to evangelize the world were not validly baptized?

Though we can applaud the desire of the Anabaptist and the Revivalist for calling people to a living faith we must also point out they err when it comes to baptism. The Scriptures are clear (Ephesians 4.5) and the creeds of the Ancient and Historic Church confirm that there is "one baptism" not to be repeated.

Bishop Craig Bates on Infant Baptism

JULY 25, 2011 The Most Reverend Craig Bates

The last few months I have been approached by several young Christians and asked to defend "infant baptism." I am not sure, however, that as a Biblical Christian I need to defend a practice that has long been accepted by the vast majority of Christians, including most Evangelical Christians. The fact is that those who support the position of "believer's baptism" as an act of obedience rather than as sacrament are in the minority. The position they take would ignore the reality that the early Church indeed baptized infants and that this practice was not only the norm but was universally practiced by all Christians until the late sixteenth century. Not only do they find themselves in disagreement with the Church Fathers like Athanasius and Augustine, who were most certainly men of Scripture, but also with the Reformers like Martin Luther and Calvin.

Those of who defend the Christian and Biblical practice of

baptizing infants need merely offer the defense that this teaching and practice is not only Biblical but is the practice of the Church from Apostolic times. Those who hold to so called "believer's baptism" are in the ones who need to defend their position. The fact is that their position originates in the post-Reformation Anabaptist movement of the sixteenth century. And, again their position has been rejected not only by Roman Catholics, Eastern Orthodox Christians, and Anglicans, but the vast majority of Churches that grew out of the Reformation.

It is correct that the Holy Scriptures does not specially command the baptism of infants nor are there any specific examples in the Book of Acts of an infant being baptized. Though we do find examples of "households" being baptized. The lack of evidence of infants being baptized can easily be explained. The Book of Acts is the record of first generation Christians all of whom were adults. It is not clear what these new converts did with their children.

The proponents of "believer's baptism" would suggest that infants are excluded from receiving baptism since as an infant they cannot make a profession of faith. I wonder how they would deal with the text from the Psalmist, "For you are He who drew me from the mother's womb, my hope from my mother's breasts; I was cast upon You from the womb; from my mother's womb you are My God." (Psalm 21.10-11) It is clear that in the Covenant God made with Abraham – marked by circumcision – which infants not only could be in covenantal relationship with God but were in covenantal relationship with God. (Genesis 17.10-13) It would seem strange would it not that the same God who brings infants into relationship with himself in the covenant of Abraham would now withhold that relationship from those in the covenant of Christ Jesus who said, "Let the little children come to me, and do not hinder them, for the kingdom of God belongs to such as these." (Mark 10.14) The word for here for "children" is the Greek word "paidia" which can be translated "babes in arms" or "infants".

Isn't this the very reason that many who hold to "believer's baptism" practice "baby dedications" which has little if any Scriptural support and was not practiced until late in the seventeenth century? If we want to obey Jesus and bring the "babes in arms" to Him then isn't the way to do this baptism?

There are five specific references in Scripture to the baptism of entire households.

> Peter baptized the household of Cornelius (Acts 11.14)
> Paul baptized the household of Lydia and the household of the Jailer (Acts 16.15,33)
> Paul baptized the household of Crispus, the ruler of the Synagogue in Corinth (Acts 18:8)
> And Paul baptized the household of Stephanas. (1 Corinthians 1.16)

The Greek word for "household" is "oikon" and refers to all who abide in the household including wives, slaves, servants, infants, and children. If children were excluded would not the text had read that only the adult members of the household were baptized? Would we be so naïve as to suggest that in the household of Cornelius, Lydia, the jailer, Crispus and Stephanas there were no children or infants?

From the beginnings the Church Fathers – those closest to the actual events of the Scriptures and often the disciples of the Apostles – related baptism to the covenantal act of circumcision. In Colossians 2.9-12, Paul compares the effect of baptism to the effect of circumcision, which took place at eight days old. And, we can see in reading the Father's that the practice of baptizing children and infants was a common practice as early as the later part of the first century – Apostolic times.

What about the text in Mark 16.16, "Whoever believes and is baptized will be saved." Or, the text in Matthew 28.19-20, "Go therefore and make disciples of all the nations, baptizing them in the name of the Father and of the Son and of the Holy Spirit, teaching them to obey all things that I have commanded you, and lo, I am with you always, even to the end of the age."

The proponents of "believer's baptism" would argue that these texts should be read chronologically. That is, they would suggest that one must first believe and then be baptized. They conclude, that since an infant is not able to "confess their faith", because they have not reach an age of reason, they cannot be baptized. Hence they are excluded until reaching a proper age. The problem is that these texts are not to be read chronologically since the verbs "believe" and "baptized" are participles. So, as a person who was baptized as an infant I can legitimately say, "I believe, and I have been baptized." Matthew 28, the Great Commission, says that we make disciples or followers of Jesus through "baptism" and "teaching". Does teaching necessarily follow baptism? Of course not! They are not chronological. If the issue were chronological, i.e., "believe, confess faith, be saved, and then be baptized", the text in Mark would have to read, "Whoever believes and is saved will be baptized."

Baptism is an act of grace that precedes faith. Ephesians 2.8-9 reads, "For by grace you have been saved through faith, and that not of yourselves, it is the gift of God, not of works, lest anyone should boast." Salvation is not an act of man, certainly not of man's reason or intellectual consent, but an act of the love, mercy, and grace of God. Both faith and grace are works of God into the sinful, stubborn, and prideful heart of humanity. Can we deny that the God who gives the most arrogant and hardhearted man the faith and grace to be saved would deny that same grace to an infant? Faith is a glorious gift of God given by the Holy Spirit. Certainly an infant who has been baptized will need to receive and respond to the grace given to them throughout their entire lives. And, for some that will be a "dramatic" or "profound spiritual awakening". But the gift of grace always precedes the gift of faith.

I would suggest that those who hold to "believers baptism" have falsely placed the emphasis on the response of man rather than the grace of God. They will over and over again talk about how "they went forward", "they made a decision" and "they got saved" rather than on the marvelous and life transforming grace of God found in Jesus. They falsely argue that we are "saved by faith through grace" not as Paul so clearly and accurately taught, "we are saved by grace through faith". Should we not bring our infants under the grace of God? Then certainly we must face our parental responsibility to teach our children the truth and train them to "walk by faith."

I do not deny the reality that many people, including myself, came to a transforming moment in their life when their relationship with Christ Jesus came alive. They went from having the faith of their parents and church family to having a faith of their own. For many, this moment in time so transformed them that they were set free from the bondages of alcohol, sexual promiscuity, drug addiction and other life controlling problems or sins. Indeed, every Christian should be in a personal relationship with Christ Jesus as their Lord. But is this a failure of their baptism? Or is this a failure of the Church and families to lead our children to such a personal relationship? Isn't the most powerful "testimony" of God's love a person who can say, "I have always known Christ as my Lord and Savior?" Yes, I believe the Church needs to be active in awakening people to the reality of the Risen Christ and a life lived in the power of the Holy Spirit. But this doesn't negate infant baptism.

There is no question that the Church has over the centuries misused the sacrament of baptism. There is no question that many have been baptized out of superstition. It is also sad that many parents fail to teach their children the things necessary to walk in the truth or nurture them in the knowledge and love of the Lord. It is a sad fact that there are "baptized persons" all around us that have never come to a living relationship with Jesus nor known the joy of being filled with the Holy Spirit. This is not because they were baptized as infants. How many have made "altar calls" or gone to crusades to "make a decision" and have fallen from the faith? We need remember the teaching of Jesus in Matthew 13.1-19,18-23.

The early Christians, who saw Scripture as their authority, were clear that infants were not to be excluded from baptism for to do so would exclude them from the grace of God in the sacrament as well as exclusion from initiation into the household of God, the family of God, the bride of Christ, and the Body of Christ.

The Supreme Court of the United States and now legislators around the world have declared that infants in the mother's womb are not persons. Therefore these precious infants, who are formed and created in the mind of God for His purpose and plan, are denied the basic God given rights of life, liberty and the pursuit of happiness.

They are excluded from the community of man. Mothers and fathers have been deceived into believing that life begins at some man-determined time and therefore they can destroy the life of their child. It seems to me, now more than ever, that as the Church we continue to administer the Biblical and historic practice of baptism to infants and so affirm the truth that all life is sacred from fertilization to natural death. Baptism not only conveys the incredible and scandalous grace of God but also strengthens the family and the household of God.

The Most Reverend Craig Bates is the Patriarch of the International Communion of the Charismatic Episcopal Church, the Primate of the Charismatic Episcopal Church of North America, Bishop Ordinary of the Diocese of the Northeast, and Rector of Cathedral Church of the Intercessor in Malverne, New York.

Made in the USA
Charleston, SC
11 January 2012